The Unseen Veil

By Jasmine Beverley

First Printed in United Kingdom 2022

Published by Conscious Dreams Publishing
www.consciousdreamspublishing.com

Edited by Daniella Blechner and Elise Abram

Typeset by Oksana Kosovan

ISBN: 978-1-913674-90-8

Dedication

I am dedicating this book to women. All women. Women I know. Women I can never know. Believers, non-believers, mothers, wives, daughters, and sisters. This is my story, a chapter in my life. It is a chapter I want to share to encourage, support, and share knowledge on the truths about relationships, marriages, African mentality, the Church, and emotional abuse.

Contents

Introduction

I am writing this book to help women who have never had a voice, women who have been silent, and those who have stayed silent. Throughout this book, I address my marriage, expressing the emotional abuse I suffered, my thought processes, and my journey toward healing.

It is amazing that a new wind is blowing, and there are strong female voices who are not ashamed of what they have been through. They are owning and taking control of their stories. Young or old, women are standing up and speaking out about emotional abuse, an abuse that is unseen. An abuse that can so easily leave victims trapped and silenced.

Writing this book, I began to realise that although women are now speaking up, there are a lot of women that remain silent, feeling trapped and caged. Unfortunately, many women stay in abusive relationships due to the fear of what others may say or think, or a fear of the Church. My aim is that this book will not only comfort my fellow women, but it could also help pastors, leaders, or individuals to better understand the issues in emotionally abusive relationships.

As I write this book, I wonder how I might possibly give a voice to women, victims, and survivors of emotional abuse, the abuse that is hard to define, and unfortunately, often extremely common in marriages or relationships. The only way is for me to be a voice and share my story.

It is time for situations to change, for people to hear the truth, and to understand the effect and impact emotional abuse can have on individuals and family members.

Unfortunately, abused women, and often Christian women, feel stigmatised when they speak out against the abuse in fear of judgement from those who should understand. If a woman speaks up, she is stigmatised. If a woman tries to leave the marriage, she is condemned. This book details the issues I faced in my situation and how I overcame them. Revelation speaks about overcoming by the word of your testimony, and through this book, I have overcome.

Women with anxiety, depression, and mental health issues are finding the strength to say no to this unseen abuse. Emotional abuse is a very isolating experience, and thus, this book aims to be of help to other survivors.

I share this book so we really do know that we can speak up and not be ashamed, or even worse, silenced. I have a desire to end the cycle of silencing and blaming women for things they did not do or cause.

I am grateful and excited that you are reading this book; another woman reading is another woman empowered. Thank you for being a part of a growing, powerful, influential group of women who will speak up against emotional abuse. Let's continue to speak up, share our stories, and empower each other.

Chapter 1

A Happy-Sad State

'You will never ever ruin my 2021,' is what I said to him on the first of January 2021, at 12:05 a.m.

The room was filled with loud music. Happiness, joy, love and excitement flowed through the room with the anticipation of starting a new season, a new chapter, a new year. Families everywhere were celebrating that beautiful moment, a time to start afresh, a time to make New Year's resolutions and goals for a positive change. I had just gone upstairs after crying my eyes out, wondering where to go in the middle of the night. I was 36 weeks pregnant and holding my stomach as I walked. I had said it clearly into his ear, the anger tinged with excitement that this would not be my life. I refused to be yet another victim of emotional abuse. He would not ruin yet another celebration for me. He would not treat me badly and get away with it anymore. I will be set free. I will be okay, and I will be happy.

After saying those words, I jumped and leapt, elated at the prospect of my new start. I started dancing. I was not happy; I had chosen to be happy. I had chosen that even as he sulked and portrayed me as having hurt him and 'done him wrong' that I was going to be happy. I would not let him bring me down and shift the blame on me anymore, not again, and especially not on that day.

The start of a year is a new beginning. My baby would be due in a few weeks, and I could not continue to cry and suffer in silence. I had to make the decision to be happy, to choose life and happiness and to choose it in abundance.

He was upset with me, I was upset with him, and we were not on good terms, but all in all, we still went to church. When we arrived, I made the decision that I was going to be happy; he had made the decision that he was going to be sad. I since learnt, it is a typical trait of narcissistic behaviour, playing the victim when he was not the victim. He was down, eyes sad, head low, hoodie up, and he sat at the back of the church. Everyone knew there was a problem, that there was an issue between us. Due to social distancing, we sat far apart. For this, I was grateful. *Thank God*, I thought. What would it have been like if we had to stand together? What might the looks on our faces be? How awkward would it have been between us? What depressing energy were we projecting?

He was seated behind me, and I could feel he was not happy. I felt the dark mood, the dark air between us, the upset, the anger. I felt it all. It didn't matter that we were in church; I could still feel it.

When the time came to count down and wish each other 'Happy New Year', I – heavily pregnant – stood up, not knowing who to turn to first. I looked to my left and my right and said, 'Happy New Year' to those around me. The pastor of the church, Pastor Daniel, came up to wish me a Happy New Year, and I wished him the same back. He told me to say 'Happy New Year' to my husband. *What's the point? He is not happy, and he will not be happy until he has made sure I know he is unhappy with me*, I thought. Humbly, I walked over to him and gave him a hug. He didn't hug me back.

'Happy New Year,' I said. Of course, he still was not happy – what could I do? The fact that he was upset in the church was obvious, so I walked away and greeted those near me.

A deaconess at the church approached me, telling me again to go to my husband to say, 'Happy New Year.'

Seriously? I thought.

His approach was working. People saw him as the victim. Why couldn't anyone just tell him to say, 'Happy New Year' to me and give me a hug? To embrace me, come to me, and love me?

Heavily pregnant and due in a few weeks, I went over to him again. 'Happy New Year,' I said.

Silence.

I could not tell if I could not hear him clearly, or the face mask was stopping the sound waves, or if, in fact, he had said anything.

A few seconds passed, and he finally told me he was not happy. He explained that he wanted to talk privately, so we went to the toilet, and he told me why he was hurt.

It would be Mum's birthday in a few days. Earlier that day I had gone downstairs to take pictures with her for a mini photoshoot in our house. After we had taken the pictures together, Mum had taken some of me, and then *he* came downstairs. He was not happy because I hadn't told him I was taking pictures, and he felt as if I was leaving him out.

It had been intentional, but I didn't tell him that.

'Oh, come on – it's a new year; can't we just move on for the sake of it being a new year? Can't we just start afresh?' I said.

'I'm not happy about it,' he replied.

'Why did you even bother to come to church if you were going to be in this mood?' I asked.

'We need to resolve it now,' he continued to explain why he was not upset, 'I feel like a stranger; you don't include me in anything.'

When he came downstairs, Mum had called him over to join me in the pictures, which he did. Since I was pregnant, these were the first pregnancy photos we took together. We smiled and he laid his hands on my stomach. Mum kept taking more photos, she was enjoying it. This was really a pregnancy photoshoot. She told us to do something different 'move this side Nick...come to the front Jasmine...stand behind her Nick...Jasmine come this way,' she continued excitingly. These moments are usually nice for couples, but for us it felt strange. I felt strange. It

12

was not true happiness. I didn't feel the joy that most new mothers in a happy relationship are supposed to feel.

'Nick, can we put it behind us please?' I asked.

All I wanted to do was crawl up into a ball and cry. I had already cried so many times, and it was all I knew to do. My eyes watered. My hands shook. My heart pumped faster as the emotions drew near.

We left the bathroom. Going back into the church, I didn't know what to do. It was fake. Everything was fake. I was not happy. I was in a place where I should be able to let out my emotions, cry, be vulnerable and weak; however, I didn't know what to do. No one understood what I was going through. I looked and seemed normal. No one knew the pain I felt.

It was horrible. Sadness consumed me as I climbed down the stairs to the church's exit and went outside. It was pitch black. The night was dark. There was not a star in the sky to be seen. In fact, all I could see was clouds shrouded in darkness. Complete silence. I tried opening my eyes, only to realise they were already open. Most night skies are the darkest of grey, but this one was pitch black. It was as if someone had turned off the stars and the moon.

Where should I go? I was carrying a baby and was heavily pregnant, so I couldn't go far.

What should I do? I needed an escape. Not a physical one – because, you know, life – but something to get me out of my head. Looking back, I realised that no one had followed me, no one had come to check to see if I was okay, no one had cared to see where the pregnant lady had gone. No one knew a thing.

I went back inside and sat on a seat. Everyone else was still upstairs, dancing for joy and for the beginning of the new year. I, on the other hand, sat downstairs with tears of pain running down my face.

In an effort to reach for help, I called my friend, a deaconess at the church, to come downstairs, but the phone rang and rang. I knew she probably couldn't hear it with the excitement and loud, joyful music, and she probably wasn't holding her phone.

I decided that I had cried enough. I had shed enough tears. I had to think about my baby. This is a new year, Jasmine, I told myself. Go back upstairs. Rejoice. Be happy. Don't let him put you down and ruin yet another special occasion.

I walked upstairs, wiping my tears, my head held high.

As I entered the room, I saw him. He was still at the back, still looking sad. I thought, I'll use this time to say those important words of which I am still very proud. I said: 'You will never ever ruin my 2021.'

Back home, after the service, he still sulked, and we hardly spoke. That was it: a deafening silence between us.

Chapter 2

Don't Look

It was a simple question, a question that had come out of distrust, uncertainty, and fear; I asked him why he'd deleted the videos from his YouTube history.

'Oh, that's what I do,' he replied.

'But why?' I said.

It was Tuesday afternoon, a nice sunny day; I was on maternity leave and our baby boy was less than one month old. He had shift work and was off today. With nothing much to do together indoors, we were looking for a movie to watch.

'Can you stop ruining a good time? We're supposed to be looking for a movie!' he exclaimed.

'I delete the videos I won't watch again,' he said.

'Yes, but why?' It did not make sense to me. Why would you delete videos from your YouTube history unless you had something to hide? I know he was deleting the video trailers, no big deal, right? However how he did it was automatic. As if it was something he did on numerous occasions. I was not in a great mood because he had not clearly answered my question, which left me feeling uneasy, curious, and suspicious.

That was the problem. He never answered questions properly, he was never honest, and I had my doubts.

He was not happy that I had asked him the question. 'Why would you ask me that?' he said.

I had asked him the question because a few weeks earlier, I'd been looking for a video I had previously watched in my YouTube history, and I was surprised to come across five videos that had been watched that day. It was the content of the videos that had shaken me. One was of a lady swimming in the lake. The title was 'The Most Beautiful Woman, Swimming in the Lake'. The second video was a man and woman barely dressed, kissing and touching. The title wasn't in English. The third video was similar, and I didn't open the fourth one. I did not watch these videos on YouTube, and although it was on my phone, I figured our accounts must have linked. When he got back from work that evening, I asked him about the videos.

'I didn't watch them,' he said.

He brought out his phone and showed me his YouTube history, which contained only football highlights. He flicked through it, showing me everything he had watched recently. Football. Football. Football. Every single one.

So, that was where the question had come from. He'd searched for a movie to watch, he'd deleted the trailers from his history and I became suspicious as to why. He was not happy I'd asked and we argued that evening. Things had got so bad, there seemed to be no resolution in sight.

'I'm going to call Pastor Daniel,' he said.

'Okay, fine,' I said, though I was frustrated he had to get involved.

He called Pastor Daniel and we both tried to explain what happened. There was no real resolution on the phone and, before we knew it, Pastor Daniel was outside the house knocking on the door. Bless him. He wanted to help and make peace between Nick and I. Mum had opened the door and he walked upstairs to our room.

'Please, stop asking him questions and checking his phone,' Pastor Daniel said to me. I was rather confused at this response. I thought this comment was unfair. I know he just wanted Nick and I to be at peace and I can imagine him thinking that if the phone is causing problems, then I should stop looking.

'I don't check his phone,' was my response.

At the beginning of the year, I decided not to go anywhere near his phone. I did not want to see anything that would upset me, like the time I went into his history and saw porn websites.

'Many marriages break up because the wife checks the husband's phone,' our pastor continued.

I grew more upset because my husband sat there with his shoulders squared. 'Yes, don't question me,' I imagined him saying.

As soon as Pastor Daniel left, it got worse. He did not say a word. He sat there, on his phone, holding it up to his face, knowing I had been instructed not to question him about his viewing habits. I could not stand him. I was so distressed; I was filled with anger and rage. What was I doing in a marriage like this? One in which there was no real communication, one in which the man overpowered the woman, one in which the woman sat back and did not question her husband, one in which the woman was expected to stay silent?

I cried. Tears poured down my face. He just sat there on his phone in silence. He did not say a word.

Holding our baby in my arms, tears trickled down my face. Blowing my nose and wiping my face, I continued to cry. Feeling lost and confused, I felt there was no one to speak to about how I was feeling. No one to understand.

I cried for 30 minutes whilst he sat there in his own world, absorbed in his phone. When I couldn't take it any more, I left the room and went straight into the bathroom, holding our baby in my arms. I closed the door. Sitting on the floor behind the door, I felt like an alarm clock, constantly ticking, waiting for someone to switch me off. There I was, sitting on the bathroom floor, crying with my son in my arms. It felt like I had been sucked into a deep, dark, black hole, never to be seen again. My world had been turned upside down. The situation was toxic, and it was damaging. I sat and pondered what was happening. Had I become a wallflower, a colourless, forgotten wallflower that had given all of my colour and light away? Maybe I had been camouflaged and was no longer recognisable.

My mum was upstairs, and she had seen me go into the bathroom. 'Jasmine?' she called to me.

I came out and went downstairs. I heard her go into our bedroom to speak to Nick. I do not know what was said, but he soon rushed downstairs to see me.

When I saw him, I thought he came downstairs to comfort me. Then he started speaking. He looked innocent as always, but I saw behind the innocent look. I saw the smirks, the pride, the ego. He came straight up to me and looked me dead in the eyes. Expecting him to comfort me, apologise AND tell me it was okay, I waited for him to start speaking.

'Jasmine, you really need to stop asking me questions,' he said. His voice was soft and calm. 'If you had never asked me that question, this would not have happened,' he continued.

It wasn't unusual that I was being blamed for the issue and the argument. It happened every time. It just took me by surprise.

'Can't you just leave me alone, please? Why do you like to bring me down when I'm already down?' I asked him. 'Instead of lifting me up, you bring me down – do you like seeing me sad?'

He didn't respond, but he did continue to explain to me why I was wrong and why *he* was the one who was not happy.

'You have hurt my feelings, don't you know?' he said.

'How? How did I hurt your feelings?'

The situation always seemed to divert to *his* emotions and how *he* was feeling.

As I listened to him explaining how I offended him and how I make him feel uncomfortable, I couldn't control my anger.

'Can you stop telling me I'm wrong? Why don't you do what the Bible says and take the speck out of your own eye. I cannot always be wrong!' I exclaimed.

I was fed up. The blame-shifting was driving me crazy. He was skilled at understanding my insecurities and vulnerabilities and he would tailor his tactic or approach to destroy the foundation of who I was and my self-worth. I was fed up with constantly being told I was doing a multitude of things wrong.

That night, when I put the baby to bed, Nick and I did not speak. The next morning, he tried to speak to me, but by that time, I was still emotionally drained, exhausted, and sad.

It was not long before he continued to let me know it was my fault: 'All you needed to do was not ask me that question, and we wouldn't be here right now with this problem,' he said.

'Nick, please, just leave me alone. Please, please, please,' I responded.

I ran back into the bathroom, my safe place. Deep emotions had been stirred up, and there was no other outlet but through my long-lasting sobs. My eyes screamed with pain, and I cried out in a loud, shaky voice, 'I'm always wrong, I'm always wrong.'

It was one month postpartum, I was still weak, and I was still bleeding. Blood dripped between my legs, and I was distressed, sad, and angry, and I screamed and cried. I could not contain my anger.

He came into the bathroom and told me to calm down. 'It's fine. It is okay,' he said. I looked at him and saw that he had no emotion. Did he not care? It was a question I had asked him so many times before. It was as if he felt joy and deep satisfaction when I was upset or crying knowing that his behaviour had affected me. Being made to believe that everything was my fault had taken its toll on me. I was becoming so used to it that I started believing it myself. It was only later that I realised, in the marriage, I had done many things right. There were times I had resisted falling victim. There were times I'd said no to the abuse. I had been pregnant, and I had kept myself and my baby safe. Nevertheless, at that moment, I believed I was in the wrong.

It was like pouring salt on a wound. It felt like I was being pulled down repeatedly.

I agreed I would never look at his phone or ask questions again. I could no longer be bothered to make my marriage a success. It was fake. Why was I suffering? Why was I down? I wondered why women stayed in marriages that brought them down. Why stay in a sad marriage? Why stay in a marriage where you can't speak or voice your opinion in a relationship you fear? Why agree to live in silence?

Love.

Many women stay due to love or fear, fear of what people – or the Church – might say. Oh, I was not fearful at all, but I don't know why I didn't leave sooner.

Whilst I sat thinking about marriage and relationships, I thought about the women at my church. Most of them came to church without their husbands or spouses. A common prayer point I would hear some women say is that they were praying for their husbands to come home. Where had they gone? Why had they gone? What was going on with men? What was going on with the husbands of the women at church, and why was it a common prayer point? These thoughts would churn over in my mind again and again.

To be seen and adored for who I really was had proven difficult. It was often difficult for him to see who I really was because he only focused on himself. His emotions were always more important and superior to my own.

A year earlier, I had been ordained as a deaconess so I wasn't surprised by his response when I explained to him I was leaving the marriage. 'You can't leave. You're a deaconess at church. You're a leader – what would people say? What would your friends say?' he said.

I paused as I thought about it. Surely what they would say could not be worse than the dynamics of the marriage.

'To be honest with you, Nick, I don't care,' I responded, my voice shaken. 'I don't care what people think or say.'

At that point, I was fed up. I was being manipulated, emotionally abused, and controlled. I explained to him that I would rather have everyone see me as a bad wife who had left her marriage than be seen as a good wife but dying inside. It felt like a time bomb was ready to explode. I wasn't going to explode. I was going to be set free. I would be free to tell my tale. Although I didn't know this at the time, that indeed in the unforeseeable future I will be truly free. The uncertainty of leaving him unnerved me. How would my life be if I left the marriage? How will I pick up the pieces?

I constantly wondered if things would ever change? As a strong believer, I held onto the thought that things would change and be better, and that was God's will for my life, that all would be well. Imagine living through five years of that with no difference. Seven, eight, ten years, and still no difference. Then, imagine 20 years of suffering before I finally left. How would it look then? How would I feel? Wouldn't I wish I'd left earlier? It's not that I was living in fear – I was being hopeful and optimistic that things would change and accepting that for the time being, I would be emotionally drained.

***

My pregnancy had been hard. I had 24-hour nausea. They do not tell you that morning sickness is not just in the morning. I was sick in the morning, the afternoon, the evening, and at night, multiple times a day. I had sudden, intense urges to vomit, with the overwhelming sensation that throwing up would make me feel better but in fact it would often make me feel worse. The abdominal pain was intense, and the dizziness and continual feeling of sickness was more than I could cope with. Surely, there had to be something that could help.

I called the doctor, eager to hear a solution.

'Well, just know baby is fine,' Doc said.

'So, there isn't anything that will help?' I was shocked by his reaction and that indeed this was normal.

'If it is really that bad, we can prescribe you anti-sickness tablets,' he said.

Yes! I thought. Finally, I was happy. Finally, there was a cure for the sickness.

I was excited when he prescribed the tablets. I rushed to the pharmacy to collect them. Initially, it seemed okay, the sickness tablets stopped me from vomiting, but I still felt incredibly sick. The feeling of nausea stayed, and was worse now because I was not actually vomiting. The tablets also made me extremely drowsy and I would occasionally fall asleep whilst working. Thank God I was working from home. I took the tablets for seven days, Somehow, I got through. It became challenging when Mum cooked certain foods in this house. It seemed my sense of smell had heightened. The smell of different foods made the nausea worse and often left me feeling lightheaded and dizzy. Chicken was the worst. The smell was horrible. I couldn't stand it. I realised it was not just the food, it was my scented toiletries and cleaning products. I knew the sickness was getting out of hand when the air outside also smelt. It was strange to me. How can the air smell? Later, I realised, thanks to Google, that it was indeed normal.

Everything took me by surprise. I had no idea pregnancy could have all these effects on the body. Unfortunately, it seemed I had all the worst symptoms pregnancy could offer. I was not ready for any of them.

My tastebuds had now changed. It seemed everything made me feel sick. I didn't know what to eat anymore. It was literally trial and error to see which foods would stay down and which would trigger the nausea. I would wake up and drink Coke which I never usually drank. Coke was the only drink that eased the sickness. It became my medicine.

As pregnancy made its changes on my body, it also affected my mind, my thoughts, and my emotions. Great.

***

It was in the early hours of the morning. We had been talking all night – or rather, I had been talking all night. I was trying to explain to him how I had been feeling and what was going on physically – mentally. Though I was constantly sick, we had been arguing literally every day. Even though each day presented a new and different argument, they all seemed to connect, whatever the situation was it would always end up being extremely difficult to resolve. He commonly shifted the attention from the issue to accusations about my character and what he perceived to be my flaws. A situation would occur and no matter how big or small, it would leave me in tears every single time. I would be blamed for the disagreement or blamed for how I made him feel. I explained to him how I thought he should treat me now that I was pregnant and running low on strength.

'I would appreciate if you could overlook things because I know my hormones have changed and I am sometimes very emotional,' I said. I went on explaining the female body. I explained that the changes in my emotions were similar to the way I had gone off certain foods.

His response was heart-breaking: 'You are not the first one to be pregnant, and you will not be the last one to be pregnant neither. Is it your pregnancy that's making you act like this?'

Oh, the rage and anger! I was disgusted. This was the man I called my husband.

'You are my husband, Nick; can you try to understand what I am saying? It's not been easy for me and I really would like your support.'

'I don't understand. You cannot blame your pregnancy,' Nick responded.

Pregnancy should be treated with care, respect, and love, I thought, *maybe he does not know that yet.* I couldn't believe my ears, but for some reason, unknown to me, I continued to defend my case trying to make him understand how difficult my pregnancy was.

'That does not make sense! Can you hear yourself? You said pregnancy is affecting your emotions, you sound crazy,' he responded.

'YES!!! It is affecting my hormones, my emotions, everything. Can you try to at least understand?' I said now even more angry.

'But you need to understand how I'm feeling,' he said in a quiet voice. 'You are overreacting about everything. You are delusional,' he responded.

It was at that point tears started to pour down my face.

'Here we go again, now you are crying,' he said.

'How can you say that?' I said sobbing.

He didn't respond. He just lay there before turning to face the wall.

'I'm tired I need to sleep,' he responded.

I continued to cry until I fell asleep. Desperate and isolated, I wondered if it would always be like this. This feeling started to become all too familiar. I was used to this. I was used to being misunderstood and unheard. I guess you were wondering if it had always been like this. It was.

Before my pregnancy, we argued, day and night. The arguments always seemed very petty but would always seem to explode very quickly into an extremely big issue. The first main issue was he had completely changed. He was different to the man I had known during our courtship stage. The man that told me repeatedly that he loved me, that he wanted to see me happy and would do everything to always keep a smile on my face. He was different, and the change happened almost overnight. *Where did the original Nick go?* I wondered.

Chapter 3

An Unseen Veil

I wanted to marry a man after God's heart. I didn't have a list, a type, but that was something I wanted, something to which I was attracted – a godly man. I was not fussy about anything else. If a man had a heart for God, then that was perfect. I wanted a man who would long for a closer relationship with God, someone who would cleave to pray and be in His presence, to hold hands with me in prayer, who would cry out to God in honesty, asking for mercy and peace. A man who would plan his day and let God direct, would surely be a good man. That was what I had prayed for; that was what I longed for. Surely that man would look after his wife, treat her right, and cherish every moment with her? Well, it was not like that at all.

Before we got married, during our courtship, Nick called me every night to pray without fail. There was never a day he didn't call. Wow, this is awesome! He wanted to pray with his soon-to-be-wife, putting God at the centre of our relationship, joining hands together in prayer. I was happy. It was all I wanted. Sometimes, he would call, and I wouldn't want to answer. I was tired, but I knew the routine: we prayed quickly, and then I could sleep. After we got married, the praying had stopped. It seemed to have vanished in an instant. It was only later I realised he had mirrored me, mirrored my interests, values, and idea of how a good Christian man should be.

Before marriage, we used to tune in to Pastor Daniel's morning prayers. He would tune in at his house, and I would tune in at mine. I was always happy when I saw his name, Nick, watching live with me. When we got married, and we were together, that stopped – or should I say it never started.

'Do you want to do Bible study?' I would ask.

He would respond with 'later', or 'tomorrow'. We used to end up arguing because he didn't want to do Bible study. 'Is Bible study all we'll be doing?' he would ask.

Nick had seemed like a religious man and had expressed that when we were married, we would study the word of God together which I was extremely happy about because that is what I wanted. However, when we got married and he did not want to study the Bible, it became a big issue. I was confused.

'Why did you marry me?' I asked. 'Why didn't you marry a non-religious girl?' I was perplexed with the fact we were arguing about reading the Bible together.

He didn't respond; he simply laughed. Everything seemed to be a joke.

It was a question I'd asked on several occasions, and it was only a thought, but had he married me to exercise his entitlement?

Although he was calm, reasonable, and rarely raised his voice, the look on his face and the tone of his voice, soft but firm and incredulous, made me feel helpless and out of control. When he told me to watch my tone, I felt controlled and belittled.

I was holding a mug and, out of frustration, I threw it on the floor. From that day on, I was labelled as having anger issues but, in all honesty. When reminiscing on what had happened, everything I remembered, according to him, seemed to be only in my head. I was constantly doubting my own experience and the reality.

'Jasmine you really need to be careful with your anger. You have serious anger issues and it is not okay,' he said whilst holding me close.

It was becoming frustrating and infuriating when he would thrust his own weaknesses and issues that needed to be addressed onto me. He did it in a calm way, making me believe he loved me and was only trying to help.

The anger issue comments continued. He would often call Pastor Daniel and make jokes that he feared me, that I would hit him one day. That was when I realised that what I said and did would be used against me, and I made sure I would never break anything again. When anything went wrong in our relationship, he always went back to the time I'd broken the mug and used it as a weapon against me.

It was a downward spiral of emotional torture from then on. When I got defensive because he'd shifted the blame on me, he belittled my defensiveness. 'Why are you so angry?' he would say. You can imagine how this made me feel – even angrier.

I had chosen him because I believed it was God's will. I believed that he would look after me, love me, and help me grow in my relationship with God. From the very beginning, when I saw he didn't want to pray or read the Bible with me, the attraction, the reason I had married him, believing it was God's will and that he was a good man, was gone. I didn't know who he was. That was when I noticed that I didn't know everything. There was a veil, an unseen veil, that I was not even aware of. I did not love him, and it was even harder loving him, seeing who he really was. I knew how he was treating me was not right. He used to say I was the most amazing woman. Now, he treated me like I was nothing. It was hard, but the vows had been made, I was wearing the ring, that was that. He was my husband.

From my wedding day, my mind raced with thoughts, trying to understand the decision I had made but not understanding who I had made the decision with. It was a battlefield, a state of confusion, a blur.

***

'Let's start. Let's do Bible study today. We'll start with Genesis,' he said.

Yes! Wow! God had answered my prayers. It was great.

We started with Genesis 1 and continued to Genesis 2, both of us taking turns at reading one verse each. I was pleased. I smiled. It was a genuine smile, a smile I had not made in a while.

After we'd read, we spoke about the chapter. We talked about what stood out to us and what we'd received and understood from the passages. It was great, but unfortunately, short-lived. We were busy. We did Amazon deliveries as a side hustle. Newlyweds, a husband, and a wife, doing Amazon deliveries together. On a sunny day, you would think it would be fun, full of laughter, full of excitement, that we were still in our honeymoon phase.

Not quite.

The shifts were mainly silent. It was not like two best friends working and having fun together. It was more like strangers coming together to do a shift. I missed the spark, especially on the shifts. We were doing something. We were finally out of the house after lockdown had kept us in. I was happy, but the shifts were mostly dead, with a deafening silence between us as we sat and listened to LBC. The update on the number of COVID-19 cases filled our ears. My mind always raced with thoughts. Life had changed, and it was supposed to be a good change, I was supposed to be enjoying it, but it felt as if we were enduring it. We looked for the morning shifts and secured a few for the day. After one or two shifts, we came home in the early afternoon, with the day still ahead of us. In our room in my parents' house, I sat on the bed while he lay on the bed on his phone.

I asked about Bible study, and we argued again and again. *Maybe my approach was wrong*, I thought. Maybe if I just started doing it, he would join me. Maybe I needed to try a different technique.

I did. It was hard, it didn't work, and he didn't join me. The more he said he was tired in the morning because of the Amazon shifts the previous day, and he couldn't tune in to the live prayers, the more I thought about who I'd married. Why wouldn't he do Bible study with me any more? Why doesn't he want to invest in our spiritual life like he said he would in the beginning? What was this? I was confused. Who on earth did I marry? I knew Bible study was not all that we would do as a married couple, but my desire was to grow with my spouse in the things of God, serving God, and building a home. That was what I desired, and we had spoken about it several times before marriage. He would say he was excited to do Bible study with me, but all of a sudden, after we'd said the vows, things had changed. Why and how that happened, I don't know.

I prayed hard. Maybe it was my duty to bring him back to God again?

I prayed. I dedicated my mornings to praying for him to pray. A good friend of mine, a deaconess at the church, bought me a book called *The Power of a Praying Wife*. It was a powerful book with many great reviews. She said she'd read it over and over again.

I used to go for walks, read, and pray for Nick. The book was filled with my notes on all of the pages. Not only did I pray, but I wrote, too, praying for him in my writing. I read the prayer points repeatedly. I was determined that the marriage would work. I also encouraged myself in the Lord, just like David did in the Bible.

It will be okay, Jas. It will. I told myself. *You will be happy.*

'Please, let's go on a walk today,' I said.

'No, it's cold outside,' was the response. It was morning, the sun was shining, we had no plans, nowhere to go, and nothing to do. I wasn't working, he was on furlough, and we were stuck at home together.

I was upset and we sat in silence, him on his phone, me not knowing what to do, scrolling on my phone, wondering how on earth I had arrived in my situation.

'What are you doing?' I would say.

'Just watching videos,' he'd reply.

'Cool,' I said. I was shocked at how quickly our relationship had lost its love, fun, and joy. It was strange.

I gave him a list of five options, asking him to pick one thing he would like to do. 'We can read, we can bake, we can play a game, we can go for a walk, or we can cook a meal together.' I gave him these options and sat patiently as he thought about what he wanted to do. I couldn't believe I did that. The same person who had adored spending time with me, who had wanted to sit and chat with me, who would have loved to have gone on a walk with me just to spend time with me, was now the person to whom I gave options.

I looked at him whilst he considered what he might like to do. Ugh, it was a horrible feeling. The love and joy that had been there during courtship had begun to crumble into pieces. That was when I started to wonder if it had ever truly been there. Had it been real? What had happened? Asking and pleading for him to do things with me was not what I wanted to do, but now I didn't have a choice. I wanted his attention and his love again.

Sex seemed to be one thing he didn't mind doing. It got to the point where I would prepare myself to tell him, 'Okay, let's have sex.' It was the only time in the day that we would actually spend time together though we were in the same room all day. It was sad, but I tried my best to create some love between us so I would feel loved, valued, and beautiful. I longed for a compliment. Does he even see me? I was the same woman he'd admired before, but now it seemed different. He was occupied with his phone, and I was distressed. At night, the time when couples lay and talked about life, goals, and special moments, it was silence. No talking. Nothing. We were newlyweds, but we were living as if we were roommates with nothing much to say.

A month later, a month into marriage, after I stopped asking about Bible study, he joined me with evening devotions, which I valued. It was the only time we read scriptures together, and I was so grateful for these devotions. Spending the time reading through the passage, summary and questions was nice but after we did our devotionals, there was silence.

'Please, can we talk?' I asked.

'Okay. Sure,' he responded.

There was silence.

'What do you want to talk about?' he said.

I just wanted to talk with no specific topic in mind, just general talk about life or goals. I wanted to have a laugh and spend time in one another's presence. 'Not sure. You?'

'I don't know either,' he responded.

There was literally nothing between us, nothing to talk about, and nothing to share. I missed the days of our courtship, the fun times when we discussed something new every day. We were one month into marriage, and I missed having a person to talk to, someone to chat to at night, someone to have fun with, and someone to love.

So, what happened? What changed? And how did we get here? How did we end up married?

Chapter 4

The First Impression

I remember the first day I met him. It was Sunday morning. He came to my church and was ushered to sit next to me. After the service, I spoke to him. He was a newcomer, so I welcomed him to the church and spent a little more time speaking to him.

'Did you enjoy the service?' I asked.

'Yes, I did,' he responded. 'Do you come here every week?'

'Yes. This is my church. I'm here all the time.'

He told me that he'd see me again the following week. The truth was that I was not attracted to him, and I definitely wasn't thinking that this would soon be the man I'd call my husband.

The following week, he came back, but I hadn't noticed him. I worked in the technical department, so I was always sitting at the front, putting scriptures on the board and checking to see that the microphones were working.

Immediately after the service, he was there right in front of me. 'Hey, Jasmine,' he said.

Instantly, I knew he was interested. I could tell. You know how you can tell when a guy is interested in you? There's a gut feeling that you have, and I had it.

'Hi,' I said, putting on a smile. The conversation continued, starting with the service and the message. He was wearing a shirt with smart trousers, but I have to admit, I wasn't keen on his dress sense.

'So, what do you like doing?' he asked.

'Umm…I like reading, and writing,' I responded.

He kept asking me questions until it got awkward, and in all honesty, I just wanted him to leave me alone. I wanted to get away. 'Just one sec,' I said, rushing to my mum to speak to her.

'Mum, that man won't leave me alone. He keeps asking me questions,' I said.

'He is a newcomer. Go and speak to him. He doesn't have any friends,' she said.

Ah, okay, I thought. Fair enough. Maybe it was just because I was the only one he knew. I went back, not wanting to be rude. Maybe he did just want to be friends.

Nah, I knew he was interested.

I wasn't attracted to him. He looked much older than me and I didn't get those butterflies you get when you meet someone you like. Although I didn't have a type, he didn't tick any of my boxes physically.

The weeks went on, and he kept coming to church, always coming to speak to me immediately after the service. It was on the third Sunday that he came over to ask for my number. I was hesitant. It was too much, and it was going too fast. I know that if we hadn't been in church, the communication would never have continued. I gave him my number quickly, aware that he didn't have a pen or paper. To be honest, I didn't expect him to message me; I didn't want him to message me.

When I got home, I saw a message from him. I was shocked and confused at how he had managed to remember my number as I had said it so quickly. I immediately blocked him. I wasn't interested. It was too much. Something was not right, but he kept coming back to church every week to speak to me.

I started a women's group in the church called Daughters of Adonai, a group to empower and equip women of God through the Word. It was morning, and I was leaving the house for work when I saw a text message; it was him.

Having blocked him on WhatsApp, I'd forgotten to block his actual number, so there was still an avenue of communication. He asked about the woman's group, how it was going, and he sent a prayer that God would bless the ministry. Aww, I thought. This had caught my attention. I responded, and that was it.

Communication continued and he asked if I wanted to go on a date, and I agreed. I thought I would just go to see how it went. I wanted to see if we would connect. Would there be a spark? Would we laugh and joke? Would I realise he was the man of my dreams? I agreed to give it a go.

We met up at the station. He was late, so I decided to go to the supermarket to get a drink. As I was walking into the supermarket, I saw him across the road, walking up to the station. He was looking right at me, but he kept walking. I wondered if he didn't know it was me. Had he seen me? It was rather strange.

I went back to the station and saw him there. He said he didn't know that the lady walking into the supermarket was me. I didn't think much about it then, but later I realised that he had seen me and thought I was another woman, even though he was looking straight at me. This became a problem later when I realised that he looks at every woman!

I addressed him about it later, once we were officially together. 'Why do you always look at women when we're together?'

'Maybe I do it unconsciously. I don't know that I do it,' he responded.

'Okay, but you do,' I said.

'And I always look at you to see that you are not looking at other men.'

Yeah, right, I thought – *what a good response.* It was a good way to avoid what I had asked. Nevertheless, I was happy I had said it. I was happy he knew what made me uncomfortable.

When I saw him at the station, he immediately took hold of my hands. 'Sorry, I'm late,' he said. His hands were sweaty. I couldn't wait for him to let go of them. He was in my personal space. He was so close. It was too much. Why were his hands sweating so much? Maybe he was nervous.

'It's fine. No worries,' I responded. 'Let's go.'

He was going to take me to a restaurant; it was only later that I realised there was no plan. He asked me where I wanted to eat. There were restaurants in the area, and I picked one. We sat down, ordered, and were waiting for food when the intense love-bombing started.

'Jasmine, you are everything. You are my love. You are what I have been waiting for all my life,' he said. He went on to explain that I was his wife and how we had a future together. I didn't realise this was love-bombing. At the time, I had no idea, but I knew I did not like it. It was not attractive. I mean, this was the first date!

'I'm not interested,' I said.

'So, why did you come?'

'I literally came to see if we had any connection, if we could have a good time together, but no – I'm not interested any more,' I answered.

'You came because you know we have a connection,' he said. He seemed to believe that there was really something there. He went on and on, pushing me to the limit.

'I don't find you attractive,' I felt forced to say.

His response was even more shocking: 'You are looking at the physical, but you need to look at the spiritual.'

What a response!

I stopped to think. With me being a hardcore church-goer, a young lady who just wanted to do God's will, I thought about what he'd said – was I really just looking at the physical? Was I not considering the spiritual? Was there something I could not see? His response was good. I had to admit he had me thinking.

Unfortunately, he went on and on until I had had enough. My mind couldn't keep up with everything he was saying, and I just needed to leave. I finished my burger, and to be honest, I was done.

I told him I was ready to go.

He looked disappointed, but he saw I was serious. Me being me, I wasn't rude – I thanked him for the meal and for paying.

We walked back to the station. I didn't feel bad as he had pressured me, and he hadn't let the meal flow. It had felt like I'd just finished a horrible interview, and I was ready to go home.

'Please, can we get some ice cream? Please, Jasmine, please?' He literally pleaded with me. It was rather embarrassing, but he was persistent, and people were walking past, looking, and he wasn't taking no for an answer.

'No, I don't want ice cream, thank you,' I said firmly and quietly. We were now in the station and I couldn't wait for the train to arrive. As soon as it arrived, I got on and waved goodbye. I could see he was worn out. Given the look on his face as the train went by, he was disappointed. All I could think was, *phew*! Thank God that was finally over.

I called my friend to explain to her how horrible the date was. 'What was I thinking, going out with him?' I said. In the African culture, we call older men "uncle", and in all honesty, I felt I had been on a date with an uncle. I explained to my friend how it was, and I ended with, 'Never again. Never, ever again.'

After the first date, I continued to see him in church.

'Hey, Jasmine, I am really sorry about what happened. Please, give me another chance,' he said.

'Okay, you are forgiven, but I'm not interested in another date, thank you,' I responded.

Gosh, he was persistent – very persistent. I began avoiding him in church, walking in the opposite direction from him and going home before he could come up to me. The weeks went on, and he continued to try. On some occasions, when I wasn't quick enough, he would walk up to me. 'Hey, Jasmine,' he would say.

'Hi,' was my response every time.

Time went by, and I had heard he was a good man. My mum advised me, 'Jasmine, he is a good man. Give him a chance.'

Pastor Daniel also spoke well of him. Was it just me? Was I being too hard? Was he really a good man? Although I had been avoiding him, he hadn't given up – was I really the woman for him?

He kept coming to church every week. There he was, sweeping the floor, serving in the church, attending meetings. He was doing everything, and it was catching my attention. He must be a good man. Maybe this was God's will. I reconsidered and decided I would give it another go.

When I told Pastor Daniel, he was so happy and excited. 'Yes, this is God's will for your life. Nick is a good man, and he will treat you well,' he said.

I had total faith and trust in Pastor Daniel. He was a good man with a heart of gold, always wanting to help and be there for people. He prophesied that my sister would give birth to twin girls before she was pregnant, and it came to pass. I believed in him and believed he wanted the best for me, so when he said this, I was happy.

There was one thing about Nick that laid at the back of my mind, he didn't have papers, documents or the right to live in the UK. Nick was ten years older than me. He was originally from Nigeria and had lived there his entire life. He had only been in the UK for three years when we met. Initially, I wondered if he just wanted to marry me for his papers? I know a lot of men do it. Men will pretend to love a British or American woman just to marry her, get his papers and gain citizenship. Once the papers had arrived, he would leave her and enjoy his life without living in fear of immigration. The thought didn't last long, Pastor Daniel and my mum were encouraging me that this is God's will. If this is God's will the paper situation is irrelevant, right? I never thought about it again.

It felt weird, him being ten years older. However, Pastor Daniel encouraged me that 'Nick is mature, he will look after you'. I was encouraged and I guess excited too, I was walking in God's will, doing what God wanted me to do, this was all part of God's plan, I believed.

So, that's how it started. From that moment onwards, we basically prepared to get married, and the marriage counselling began. It was all very quick. Extremely quick. The courtship was about our planning for the wedding, which I believe is why we never truly got to know each other. I believe he knew me, but I never really knew the real him. I knew the 'him' who wanted to marry me. I knew the man who wanted his prize but not the man who had won his prize.

Pastor Daniel wanted to announce the engagement to the church, but my mum and my sister thought it was too quick. Mum had mentioned it to Pastor Daniel: 'This is too fast,' she explained. I could tell she wasn't happy as she had seen everything race rapidly from zero to one hundred, but I didn't really know how I felt. I just knew that if I was getting married, I wanted a nice wedding, a fairy tale wedding with family and friends celebrating with us as we celebrated the beautiful moment when two become one.

Mum and Pastor Daniel had a disagreement at one point. *Oh, dear*, I thought, *what was going on?*

'Jasmine, do you feel this is too quick? Do you feel pressured?' Jacklyn, my sister, asked me.

'I don't think so. This is God's will, right?' I was so fixated on doing God's will, fulfilling God's divine purpose for my life, and therefore, going ahead was fine with me, but deep down, there was a part of me that felt that yes, it was too quick. I didn't even know all of his brothers' and sisters' names. He must have told me, but I didn't remember; I still don't know.

Time went on, and the wedding preparations continued, including getting the rings. Things continued to go fast, and he continued to declare his love for me every single day. The constant messaging didn't stop. He would message me around 5 a.m. with a good morning text, and the messages continued throughout the day from there.

It was early afternoon, and we had planned to see Pastor Daniel, to bring the rings to him so he could pray over them and for us. Pastor Daniel was excited about what was happening, the joining of Nick and me, God at work. He said he was proud and happy.

Pastor Daniel prayed over the rings and gave them to Nick. To my surprise, he told Nick to practise. Nick was shocked, but he listened. He went down on one knee and declared his love for me in front of Pastor Daniel and myself. Deep down, it was awkward. I wondered how he could love me so much, so quickly, in a short space of time. After declaring his love for me, he asked if I would marry him. It was not a proposal I expected as I sat down in my casual velvet dress, tights, and small heeled flats.

I said yes, and we were engaged...unofficially, of course. This was a 'practice' no one knew about.

A few Sundays later was the official engagement. It was at church, which I thought was sweet as that was where we'd met. I was excited about it.

Pastor Daniel called me to the front. Then he called Nick up. That was the moment Nick officially proposed to me. He went down on one knee, his knees wobbling; I guess he was nervous. Everyone was looking at us. Those at the front had their phones out and were recording. The spotlight was on us. A few minutes passed, and Nick didn't say a word. It was silent. It was awkward. The assistant Pastor was holding a microphone to Nick's mouth. Maybe he was speaking quietly? No – no words came out.

Say something, I thought, but he didn't. He just looked down, holding the ring up. Again, I guessed he was nervous. Maybe he was shy. He had previously declared his love for me at the "practice" proposal at Pastor Daniel's house – why not now? The minutes went by, and it was getting more embarrassing.

A lady from the crowd shouted, 'Be a man!'

Someone else shouted, 'Let's encourage him,' and then the congregation started clapping.

I was confused by what was going on and why he wasn't saying anything. When I later asked him why he hadn't said anything, he responded with, 'I've never done that before.' This became his go-to response that he said on so many occasions about different situations.

Finally, he said the words. He asked me, 'Please, Jasmine, will you marry me?'

Pastor Daniel brought the Bible, put it under my hand, and asked Nick to put the ring on my finger.

Nick said, 'She hasn't responded yet.' Since everyone had been waiting so long for him to say something, they had forgotten that I had not actually answered the question yet. Everyone had forgotten, including me.

Pastor Daniel removed the Bible, and everyone waited for my response.

I said *yes*, the Bible was placed under my hand again, and Nick put the ring on my finger. That was it – we were engaged.

The congregation were thrilled and happy for us as it was the first church engagement. I was also happy. I was engaged to a man who I believed loved God, a man who, I believed, loved me, a charismatic man who would be my life partner, with whom I would serve God, with whom I would go on adventures and travel around the world. Although extremely nervous that it was moving extremely fast, I was excited and ready to get married.

The church congregation was excited, too. The church I was attending was an African church, predominantly Nigerian. I'm half Nigerian. My mum was born in Nigeria and came to the UK when she was 11-years-old.

'Make sure you are learning how to cook now. You need to cook for your husband,' an aunty in the church said. In African culture, we address everyone who is older than us as *aunty*. It signifies dignity and respect toward an older woman who has proven to be audacious and wise.

There weren't many young people in the church, so everyone was aunty, or uncle, of course, for the few men that came to church.

'Yes, aunty,' I responded. My mum had raised me not to talk back to my elders but to just respond with a yes even if I disagreed as it was a sign of respect. To disagree or challenge an adult would have been seen as disrespectful.

In the church, most of the older women believed I couldn't cook because I was from London and vegan, and therefore, I needed to learn how to cook not only African food but meat. I knew I couldn't cook African food, and I wasn't fussed. Although I love my Nigerian food, I had no desire to learn how to cook food with meat.

I had spoken to Nick about food. 'You know I am vegan, right?' I had said. 'So, I don't eat meat.' People often asked me if I was a *vegan-vegan*, meaning if I actually said no to meat and dairy all the time or if I picked and chose. My response was that I was a *vegan-vegan*.

I have this spirit that if I say it, I stick to it. I was not allergic to dairy or against the killing of animals, but after I had been vegetarian for a year, I decided to try veganism in 2018. I never looked back. I wanted to live a healthier lifestyle, and veganism would help me to do that, so there I was, a year and a half later, standing my ground that I was marrying him but asking him to please respect that I wouldn't eat meat.

'That's fine. I'm not marrying you for food. I'm marrying you for you,' was his response every time, and I appreciated it. *What a man*, I thought. He was great. He told me not to worry about what people would say, telling me to ignore them. 'We will learn and cook together,' he would say.

'Yes, I would like for us to cook and do things together,' I said happily.

'Of course, and me, too,' he responded.

'How will you cook meat for your husband when you are vegan, and you won't be able to taste it?' Honestly, it was very stressful and draining listening to the constant comments about what I ate, how I would prepare the rice and if I would prepare two different meals every day. The comments were becoming too much, and I was tired.

'I will manage. We will work things out,' I would respond. I hated the topic of food, my being vegan, and cooking. Whenever I realised the conversation was leaning towards that topic in church, I looked for a quick escape.

'By the time you are pregnant, you will eat meat,' they all said, including Nick.

'No, I will not,' I responded. The truth was that I didn't know. I had never been pregnant before. Even if I would have, their belief that I would eat meat made me even more determined to say no to the chicken nuggets and chocolate biscuits when I was pregnant. I was not going to let them say, 'I told you so.' No way.

The constant questions about what I would eat, how would I cook for him, would I let the children have meat amazed me. The joining of myself and Nick intrigued everyone; a girl from London, marrying a Nigerian man, a man who had lived in Nigeria his whole life, a man who had only been in the UK for three years. To be honest, I don't blame them. It intrigued me, too. It intrigued me that he would soon be my husband, my life partner, the man with whom I would have children. I never imagined it, but we plan our steps, and God directs them, right? *God surprises us in ways we can never imagine*, I would tell myself.

His constant reassuring me that he would also eat vegan food and that maybe he would try vegetarian first before going vegan made me think he was different. 'You don't have to try vegetarian food. Just eat meat. It's fine,' I would say.

'No, I want to do this for you,' was his response. Now, looking back, I had fallen for everything. I mean, he had said all the right things! I never once doubted his sincerity or considered that he was not honest; I trusted him – the softness in his voice and the look in his eyes told me that he truly loved me and would do anything for me.

We met a lot of each other's families. The wedding was in a few months, so it was important that we met the family. One week it was a member of my family, and the next, it was a member of his. It was a lot, but we got through it.

'Jasmine, try some,' he said, pointing a fork with meat on it at my mouth. We were at his aunty's house. Aunty Hannah.

'No, I'm okay,' I responded, looking at him, thinking that it was not funny. I didn't understand why he was telling me to eat it when he knew I was vegan.

'Come on, J – try it,' he continued.

And that was it. The conversation started: 'Jasmine, you know God created the animals for us to eat, right?' *Oh, here we go again*, I thought.

'Yes, I know. It's a personal decision, thank you, Aunty,' I responded. Truly, I didn't understand why people couldn't leave me alone. You do you, and I do me – simple.

'Anyway, by the time you're pregnant, you'll be eating meat. Don't worry, my brother. She will eat meat,' she said, speaking to my soon-to-be husband. The anger inside me rose at the thought that people were already planning my destiny, that somehow everyone knew what my life would soon be, that maybe they knew something I didn't know.

On the drive home, I raised the issue about the food joke. It was the first of many issues that ended in an argument. 'Why did you ask me if I wanted to eat the meat?' I asked him – not to argue but to understand what was going on in his brain and from where he was coming.

'I just wanted to see if you wanted to try it. I can't eat it and not offer some to you,' he said with an innocent look on his face.

'Yes, but you know my answer will be *no*,' I responded.

'I was just playing – can I not play?' he responded.

'Yes, but you know I don't like the topic of food, and you see what it started after with Aunty Hannah,' I said.

'Okay. Sorry. It won't happen again.'

It happened again. This time when I raised it, he told me I couldn't take a joke, that he was just playing around. The joke was not funny. It was becoming a concern that I did not understand his jokes and humour. He didn't make me laugh, and the things he said which were supposed to be funny were not. What was I doing marrying him?

On Sunday afternoons after church, a few of the congregants and leaders usually stay and talk whilst we wait for the counselling sessions with

Pastor Daniel to finish. I decided to use the opportunity to speak to my pastor's wife, Pastor Kenny, about it as it was an issue that I didn't find him funny, and his jokes were leading to disagreements. I wanted to hear another perspective.

Pastor Kenny went on to speak about her and her husband, Pastor Daniel: 'Before I married Pastor Daniel, I did not find him funny, but now he always makes me laugh, you know how funny he is.' Pastor Daniel is hilarious and always had the congregation laughing throughout his sermons.

'Really? You didn't find Pastor Daniel funny?' I said, shocked, as he really is an extremely funny man. Was my case the same as Pastor Kenny and Pastor Daniel? Would I soon be laughing at my future husband's jokes? Would I laugh until I cried?

The preparation for the wedding continued, the advice continued, everything continued. I went ahead, getting ready to marry the man who was supposed to be the love of my life.

The old school, African mentality is extremely different from what I know. It is the mentality that women need to be silent, that marriages which fail are due to women either not giving their husbands sex, talking too much, or not obeying their husbands' commands. A husband might cheat on his wife with another woman, and if the wife sought advice from family or friends, the response would be, 'when did you have sex with him last, or do you have sex with him every day?'

'You have to give him sex in the morning. Then, he won't look outside when he goes to work,' an aunty said to me. I didn't understand.

A man will cheat if he wants to cheat. A good man that loves his wife won't cheat, even if they are not having sex every day. He will be loyal and appreciate his woman, his wife, his love. A man who cheats does so because he wants to. He cheats because either he was looking or the temptation came, and he gave in. Yes, the flesh is weak, but you can resist the temptation – or was I being too naïve? I understood that women could be responsible for their men's cheating, but it is not always the women who are to blame. Later on in our marriage, when I noticed my husband watching porn, that typical response shocked and repulsed me. 'Are you not satisfying your husband, Jasmine?'

***

A lady from church was getting married. We were all going to the wedding, and I invited my best friend, Tanisha. I was excited as this would be the first time Nick would meet her. In fact, it would be the first time he would meet any of my friends. She came, and they met. Later that evening, Tanisha and I were standing together, speaking to a couple with twins. Nick came out of nowhere, grabbed her hands, and took her aside.

A couple of guys nearby said, 'Oh, she's just been taken.' I didn't know what to feel. It was embarrassing. Why had he done that?

No, actually, that's my fiancé, I thought of saying, but can you imagine how awkward that might be? How embarrassing?

Later, I walked up to them both. 'Can I stay?' I asked.

'Yes, of course,' she said, probably wondering why I'd asked that. I wondered, too – why had it been that question that had come out?

I was upset, why would he take her hands and pull her aside? And then the response from the guys nearby, how embarrassed I felt. Although I was upset, I was not going to raise it then; I decided to raise it later that night on the phone when we both got home.

'I didn't like how you took her hands. It made me feel embarrassed,' I said.

'Why didn't you tell me then?' he responded.

'Oh, I wanted to wait till after,' I said.

'No, you should have told me then,' he argued.

I couldn't believe this was turning into an argument.

'She is your friend. I don't see anything wrong with it,' he responded.

I was extremely confused by what he'd said. It did not make sense. I told him the comments that those around us had said. I explained how it was not respectful behaviour for a man to come over to take a female's hands unless, of course, there was another agenda.

He was angry I had not mentioned it earlier and angry that I'd raised the issue in the first place. 'Was this a cultural issue?' I asked him. I also asked if he would be okay if I did that to his friends, but he didn't answer the question. This was the first of many times I'd told him something with which I was not happy, and he wasn't happy either. Although I had work in the morning, we argued all night. He worked in the afternoon, whereas I worked early in the morning, leaving the house before 7 a.m. We argued and argued, and I don't think I actually slept. He could not stop explaining to me why I was wrong, why he could not say sorry because I had not mentioned the issue to him at the time. The argument continued in the morning on my way to work, and I ended up crying on the journey. I ended up crying at work. From this day forwards, I routinely had emotional breakdowns at work due to misunderstandings leading to us arguing on the phone whilst I was on my way to work. It was embarrassing. So embarrassing, in fact, that I later handed in my resignation and quit my job.

This was the man I was marrying. I was not happy, and I was ready to stop the marriage, to stop everything that was going on, so I could just enjoy the life I was having before. The issue was not settled until we took it to Pastor Daniel's office. It was the first of many issues that would be taken to his office. Pastor Daniel explained that he was wrong. He told him off. *Maybe he truly didn't know it was wrong*, I thought.

Anyway, he apologised: 'I will never do it again. I'm sorry. I love you,' he said. I never understood why he hadn't said it at first, why it had taken that long, and why we had argued about the situation in the first place. Had I pushed buttons? Did he expect me to keep quiet about things I didn't like? Did I challenge him as a man? Mess with his ego? I didn't know. I also didn't know it would be a recurring behaviour trait that would go on after our marriage, that, indeed, I should be silent and accept things as they were.

The arguments continued here and there as we planned our special day. He didn't understand the need for a nice wedding. 'It is becoming expensive,' he said.

I cried a lot during courtship, nevertheless, it was God's will, right?

We went ahead, making plans for the wedding. Wedding planning is never easy, even with couples who truly love each other, who were high school sweethearts, couples who fell in love at first sight; the wedding planning process was always challenging, I would tell myself.

Time went on, and he continued to show up at church every time. He even came to the women's conferences. He said he was coming to see me, which I found obsessive, but also sweet.

The announcements in church, the stir up to the beautiful, God-centred union of Jasmine and Nick…

We were later nicknamed Jasnick. We had become the wedding of the church, the perfect couple, the couple ordained by God, it seemed.

'You are so amazing. You are the love of my life. I don't know what I would do without you. You are everything!' he would say.

'Aw, really?' I'd often reply.

It was only later that I realised the nice comments and attention was love bombing. The beginning of the courtship stage was filled with love bombing and mirroring. It left little to no space for me to see the turmoil and red flags. Love bombing is the excessive attention, admiration, and affection with the goal of making the other person feel dependent and obligated. This was happening to me! I later realised that this was a form of psychological manipulation but at the time, it made me feel loved, cherished and valued. As the recipient, it felt good. It increased and boosted my dopamine and endorphin levels and they flew around my system making me feel like I was in love. In the beginning, when we were courting, he showered me with attention, love, gifts, and his time.

He made me feel special, needed, loved, valuable, and worthy. Looking back, it was possessive, obsessive, and filled with an overflowing fountain of poetic language. The reality was that I did not know him; I didn't even know him at all.

Looking back now, I see the signs. The signs of love bombing were there. He would show up unannounced at my house early Saturday morning.

'Mum, please tell him I am still sleeping,' I would say. Upon hearing the knock on the door, I thought, *Oh, my gosh. Seriously?* I got quickly out of bed to see him.

'I'm sleeping,' I told him.

'Oh, I just wanted to see you,' he responded. It was too much. I didn't like it, but maybe he loved me that much. I believed it was all God's will for my life. I believed this was the path I had to go down. This was my destiny, getting married to this man, a man I didn't really like.

It was not easy, and if we erase God's will from the marriage, I would not have married Nick, that I know for sure. We were completely different. In fact, we didn't vibe. We didn't have the love, the connection couples have, but he made me feel sweet, and he gave me endless attention.

Nick would buy me food and deliver it to the house. He would bring flowers and presents, and sometimes he would just sit and say he wanted to just sit with me. He gave me so much attention, which is what all women want, right – to feel valued, loved, and to be shown attention? I liked the attention, and that is probably one of the reasons I said *yes*, though at times it was too much. I did like when he brought me food and bought me flowers. I didn't see behind these acts. I thought it was sweet and loving.

I wonder why he'd chosen me. Was it because I was healthy, fit, successful, surrounded by friends, happy, fulfilled, and full of life? I woke up every morning loving life and feeling ready for all of life's adventures. Later, when reading up on emotional abuse and control, I realised I was exactly the type of person narcissistic men seek because if they can take someone like that down, then, wow – their confidence shoots through the roof.

Chapter 5

The Joining of Two

The church threw a bridal shower for me. Unfortunately, it was me against the women at the church. It was intense. The questions came by one after the other.

'Tell us your name and a bit about yourself,' the organiser said.

What? I was surprised I had to talk. I thought I would be listening and gaining wisdom and advice from all the older folks, but nope, it was the complete opposite in my case. I started to answer their questions slowly. I tried to remain calm and peaceful, but it was intense.

'I studied financial maths at university and currently work at a fashion retailer,' I said. My voice was quiet, although I was using a microphone.

'Please, speak louder into the microphone,' someone at the back said.

I brought the microphone closer to my lips, fearing the next question. I saw my sister. She was my hope in the crowd. Thank God she was there. I mouthed 'Please, come forward,' to her. I needed her closer if this was going to be an interview as to why I wanted to get married and a test to see if I was ready. I was not ready or prepared for this.

When someone raised her hand to ask me a question, the microphone would be handed to her. 'You seem shy to answer these questions – how will you cope in marriage when all the spotlights are on you?'

Honestly, I thank God for keeping me calm. 'Marriage is between two people: him and me. We will work together and do things together. I won't be in the spotlight, thank you.'

Everyone started to clap. Some whispered amongst themselves, 'That was a good answer.' I felt somewhat relieved that my answers were 'good'. I looked at my sister and gave her the eye as if to ask, 'Was that okay?' and she smiled.

Another deaconess in the church, my closest aunty, Deaconess Lydia, said, 'You are doing fine. Well done.' I drank some water, waiting for the next question.

'You said Nick likes you because you are slim and tall – when you have a baby and your body changes, how will you maintain your shape?' a lady in the crowd asked.

'My sister has managed to look good after three children. She's my inspiration. I'm sure I will be fine. I will eat healthy and live clean.' I thought my response was okay, but oh, no, it wasn't. From that moment onwards, I was told that I shouldn't compare myself to my sister, that we were different, and it was not good for me to compare myself to her.

I tried to defend myself: 'I'm not comparing myself to my sister. I'm just saying she is my inspiration. She is a mum of three, and she looks good. That's all.' It was a losing battle. Why would they put me through this when it was torture, just torture? I wanted to cry. Tears built up in my eyes, but I managed to hold them down.

The in-law questions started to come. The talk about cooking. The fact that I was vegan. It just got worse and worse.

'Nick is an African man. You are a British girl, and you are vegan. How will you cook for him?'

My response was rather shaky: 'He is not a typical African man.' I now understand that he did hold an old school, African mentality. He truly was a typical African man, and the courtship phase was a cover because he was winning me over, and he would do anything possible to get me in that phase. His old school mentality never showed, or maybe it did, and I overlooked it.

'He is an African man!' one shouted. 'Please, Jasmine, define what an African man means to you.'

My sister saw that it was getting to be too much. 'Jasmine, don't answer.' I didn't.

'Throw the question back at the crowd,' she said quietly, so I did. There was a lot of noise as the women discussed what I'd said amongst themselves, but the organiser managed to calm the crowd, and the topic changed.

A discussion that I couldn't cook followed because I was not able to cook typical African meals. The crowd concluded that I couldn't cook at all. They debated about how I would cook.

I sat there, thinking of running out, thinking of speaking up, thinking of showing how this affected me, but I was scared, and I stayed silent.

They soon brought Nick in. They gave him a chair, and he sat next to me. It was now us against them. They began to question him. The in-law questions came first, but he didn't answer the question.

An older lady in the church, who we address as Mummy Raykarn, stood up and said, 'I don't feel comfortable giving you my baby if you can't answer the question.' Mummy Raykarn always called me her 'baby'. It's a cultural thing. We were not related by blood, but I'm young enough to be her granddaughter, calling me her baby was symbolic of her welcoming me as her own…nevertheless she stood on ground trying to defend me.

At the time, I didn't understand what exactly was going on, and I didn't see why people were not happy with his responses. Yes, he'd avoided the questions, and he didn't answer clearly, but I never thought deeply about what was actually being said or avoided. It didn't occur to me that he was a character I would later be unable to deal with, a character who would drive me into depression and emotional turmoil. I never thought about this at all.

A lady at the front of the crowd said, 'Jasmine, good luck.' Had she seen something I couldn't? Had they all seen what I was getting myself into? Why hadn't anyone saved me? Why had everyone encouraged me that it was God's will for my life?

In marriage, I saw that side to Nick. It didn't take long. I saw it from the very beginning. He was good at not answering my questions and throwing them back at me. It was torture. I now understand why Mummy Raykarn had stood up in anger, fighting for me.

The questions and debate continued. It was very intense. I joined the crowd in asking Nick questions. He'd avoided so many, giving answers that didn't make sense. He later told me he'd avoided the questions because he was not going to give them what they wanted. It was his old-school, African mentality coming out, but I hadn't seen it then.

After the bridal shower, I was not happy. The embarrassment and shame put on me, the questions, the drilling – I hated it, and I cried when I got home.

A few weeks later, we drove to my sister's house, got out of the car, and as soon as we got out, ready to start walking, he stopped and brought out two packs of chewing gum. He gave one packet to me. 'Oh, thanks – does my breath smell?' I said.

He laughed, which confused me. It was genuinely a serious question, which literally needed a yes or no answer.

'No, I'm being serious: does my breath smell?' I said.

He laughed and said he didn't know. I did not find it funny. Whilst he laughed, I was confused about the situation. It was genuinely not a hard question to answer. I didn't like how he wouldn't answer a simple question. It was at this point I should have remembered from the bridal shower and saved myself from entering into a lifelong commitment with the man, but it was just chewing gum and a simple question, I told myself.

Although it was not a big issue, it later caused problems. I went to Aunty Lydia and explained the situation, and she made me see that I wasn't crazy for feeling the way I was. He should have just answered the question. I sat there listening to her, understanding that I was right to feel upset, and I wasn't over-reacting. As we sat and talked, he came towards me.

'I'm just speaking with Aunty Lydia,' I said.

He asked how long I would be, and I responded, 'Just a few minutes.' I didn't know then that finishing my conversation with Aunty Lydia and not going with him at that time would cause big issues.

He called my phone a few times, and I knew I needed to round the conversation up.

He kept calling. I didn't answer, which later became the worst decision I'd made. It was the first time we had argued in church, and it was embarrassing watching him sulk. Although sitting with Aunty Lydia and having a discussion, he was not happy that I did not answer his calls. At that point, I wasn't yet his wife, but he told me off and told Pastor Daniel that he was not happy with me.

I was fuming and upset. He didn't talk to me, and he went home with Pastor Daniel. Later that afternoon, still confused about what had happened and why he was so upset with me, I drove to his house – he lived with his two sisters and nieces. He came down to the car where it was easier to talk, and in this case, easier to argue. He explained why he was not happy, why I should have picked up my phone, finished the conversation, and seen him. We argued and argued, and he said that he didn't want me speaking to her any more. Thinking about it now, this was a red flag – a huge, red flag. She was my support system; someone I could speak to about anything. She made me feel safe, and I was no longer able to speak to her. She was the first person he'd said he didn't want me to speak to; later, it was my mum.

'If it makes you feel uncomfortable, it's a red flag.' This was a quote I'd read in an article, a year and a half later, when life had turned upside down. It's a quote of advice that I have come to cherish.

Although there were so many red flags in the courtship phase, I overlooked them in the name of God's will. I spoke with Pastor Daniel, who said he'd prayed to God and seen Nick as my husband – who was I to say it was not what I wanted? I knew I was extremely unhappy in the relationship, but I was happy I was following God's will, walking in the direction in which he had called me.

Pastor Daniel and my mum were happy, and they adored Nick, so I was happy, too. The two people I trusted and had complete faith in, were advising me that Nick was a great man and he would look after me.

Whilst there were serious red flags causing my underlying unhappiness, he was also very good at showering me with attention. After we would argue, he would express his infinite love for me and how he only wanted to see me happy. It was after we had been married that he really changed.

One of the biggest changes was attention. He no longer gave me attention. I was just there, like a biscuit on the shelf, a biscuit no one wanted to eat, a biscuit that had gone stale and got chucked in the dustbin. As soon as we were married, I'd noticed it. He no longer looked into my eyes, held my hands, and declared his love for me, telling me how much he loved me and how he would do everything in his might to make me happy. I mean, it wasn't all I wanted, and I hadn't minded him not doing it, but it was the rapid change, the immediate change that was unsettling and left me feeling isolated and lonely. The rapid difference I saw in him led me to question who I had married at a very early stage.

The praying, the activities at the church – everything had been a presentation. He had presented an idealised image of himself, an image I didn't know, and that was the man to whom I had said yes, the man to whom I was now married, but unfortunately, I didn't know him.

It was only a year later that I would come to realise his overall goal was to enhance his ego by gaining power over me by getting me to agree to marry him.

When we got married, he had me, so there was no need for the love bombing, no need for the endless attention, in fact, no need for attention at all, and it stopped completely. The arguments in our marriage were the same as those we'd had on the phone, but this time it was deeper, as we were together, we had a bond, and we were husband and wife. I noticed that my feelings and emotions were being used against me.

'You're so sensitive. You're overreacting. There you go again. I didn't do that. I didn't say that. I was only kidding. You're imagining things,' and the most common one I heard: 'It's your fault.'

It was only later I realised what it was when I came across the term *gaslighting*. Gaslighting is the invalidation and devaluation of the other party. In this case, it was me. Often, I knew in my spirit that I had read the situation correctly, but he convinced me that I had read it all wrong. As this happened, over time, my sense of reality slowly eroded away. He was aware he had control over me – I was his wife, a young girl who he had met in the church – and he thought he could treat me how he wanted. Again, this was the mentality he had that I had seen during courtship, but only a few times. Surely, this was God's will, so he will treat me right, and I will be happy, I would think. Me, being a London girl, was not going to be subjected to abuse, but I knew that mentality would not work forever. I did not plan to leave, but I knew I would not stay in a marriage or relationship where I was unhappy and abused because I was a Christian, because of the church, the family, or for their sake. I didn't know what was going to happen, but I prayed and prayed for wisdom.

The wedding day was not how we had planned it. We had planned a wedding at a venue with the bridesmaids in silver dresses and the groomsmen in dark blue suits with purple ties. The venue was beautiful, and it would have been decorated by a professional decorating company with a dazzling purple and silver theme. We had a great host, a comedian, who had done many weddings and events across the world. We also had a professional DJ who would have had the crowd engaged and dancing throughout, but the plans were put on hold. There were more cases of COVID-19, and Boris Johnson had just announced that everyone should stay home. The wedding was scheduled for March 21st, but we had to cancel it. It wouldn't be fair, putting our guests at risk. It was also likely that people would not come, and therefore, the venue would have been empty.

We postponed to an unknown date. I was upset because I had done all the planning, and it wasn't going ahead, but it could have been a lucky escape, a chance for us to really get to know each other properly, for me to see and experience the real him.

'We can just do the church ceremony and party another time,' Nick said. 'Let us continue with our plans. Let us just get married. The celebration can wait.'

I didn't like that idea. I wanted everything to be done on the same day. It didn't feel right to do half now and half later. That was not a part of the plan.

I called all the vendors one by one. They were all understanding, reassuring that it was not just us who had postponed their wedding plans. The MC said he was surprised we hadn't cancelled sooner; he thought the wedding was still going ahead. The event planner, God bless her, Aunty Natali prayed for me. She prayed that one day we would enjoy my wedding and that God's plan would still prevail.

I called Pastor Daniel to share the news. 'Is Nick aware?' he asked.

'Yes,' I responded.

'Okay, and what did he have to say about it?'

It was me who was upset and down, but that seemed irrelevant. 'He has also agreed,' I said.

'Okay,' he responded, and that was that. I wondered whether he was not happy with the decision as there had been no comfort or prayers to encourage me that all was well, and I was confused and upset.

Later that day, I laid in bed, not knowing what to do as my plans for the day had been based on our getting married that weekend. I was thinking about what to do. Nick wanted us to go ahead with the church, and I thought about it. *Just do it, Jasmine*, I thought. It doesn't matter about a fancy wedding. If this is God's will, then let's just go ahead. I didn't want to stop what God was doing.

I called Nick to explain my change of mind. He was happy, and so was I, I guess.

Our plans continued. We would not let COVID-19 and the lockdown hold us down. We would get married and start a happy life together.

My wedding day did not feel like a wedding day. I did my own makeup, and I wore braids in my hair. I wore my traditional, white Nigerian outfit; he wore the same.

The church contained less than ten people, our most intimate family members. In the morning, at home, it wasn't special, and it didn't feel special. Everything just felt like something I needed to do, something I needed to get done and tick off on my to-do list. There was no joy or excitement or butterflies getting ready. I just rushed around, getting ready for later in the day, when I joined hands with my soon-to-be husband.

Nick had been at the church with his family and Pastor Daniel. My sister also arrived at the church. Nick called me. 'Where are you?' he said.

'I'm coming. I'm just getting ready,' I replied. I was running around, putting on my eyelashes and some makeup. I mean, I wanted to look and feel somewhat pretty and beautiful.

My sister also called me. 'Where are you? We are all here.'

I again responded, 'I'm coming.'

Pastor Daniel then called, also asking where I was.

'I'm coming,' I responded. I was panicking. Everyone was waiting for me. I just needed to hurry up and get to the church, no matter what.

Finally, in the car, we were on our way. I went with my mum and stepdad. The car journey was rather strange. I was nervous. I couldn't believe it was my wedding day. I couldn't believe I was on my way to get married. I thanked God for the beautiful day ahead. I thanked God for what He was doing.

The message spoken at the church was great. It was about our marriage standing when all else failed. It was perfect for the time in which we were getting married, a time of uncertainty, loss, grief, and disappointment. It was the beginning of the lockdown, the beginning of something new.

The service was short, 45 minutes in total. After the service, we had non-alcoholic beverages whilst we took pictures. Looking at the pictures after, I didn't like them because I didn't look happy. My smile didn't look real. It was a smile I'd put on. Maybe I was nervous.

We took more pictures outside the church. I was smiling in those pictures, and it was a genuine smile. Maybe the sun had an influence. It was a nice, sunny day, and I was glad the service was over, I guess. I was also glad to be outside of the building.

Pastor Daniel took us aside. 'So, you are both married now – congratulations. You can now consummate the marriage.'

We both laughed. I knew that would happen. I knew it wouldn't be long before I'd open my legs for him.

Due to the lockdown, we had booked an apartment where we could stay for a short 'honeymoon'. We entered the room. *It was okay*, I thought, but not where I would have dreamed I would have a honeymoon. I didn't like the cream carpet; it looked dirty and had stains.

He lay on the bed. So did I.

He asked if we should have sex.

'Okay,' I said.

'Married, now, huh?'

I could no longer say no. I laid there, not knowing what to do, giving up my body for him to do whatever. A few minutes later, and that was it. He had finished, and then he slept. It was like the sleep you do after an exam, a sleep of relief. It was at that moment that I wondered what I had done. There was no, 'I love you so much,' 'We are finally married, wow,' which I assume is what people say when they just get married. There was nothing; it felt weird and strange.

It was at that moment I wondered what I had done. It wasn't long before I started to cry. It was something I had not told anyone, that I cried on my wedding day. I cried because I was not certain I had done the right thing. I cried because my life had changed, and I feared what would happen. I cried and cried.

He didn't hear me; the cry was silent. I didn't make a sound.

My mum came by in the evening to drop off some food. He was still sleeping. I took the key and went to get the stuff she'd dropped off. I wiped my tears, but I couldn't help it. I was devastated.

I got into the car and cried some more.

She sat there. 'What is wrong?' 'Was it how he touched you?' Maybe she thought I cried because I'd had sex with him, but that wasn't it.

I cried and cried, and she comforted me and consoled me and said that all was okay.

When I was done, I wiped my tears completely away. 'Do I look like I have been crying?' I asked.

'No, you look beautiful,' she said.

We called Nick to come to help with the items in the car. He came down. I got out of the car to meet him and told him that he was sleeping, so I came down first. As I spoke, I wondered if he would see my tears, if he would see that I had just been crying, but he didn't notice. The supposed love of his life had been crying, and he hadn't noticed. It was the first of many cries that he didn't notice. Who had I married? Who was he? He wasn't who I thought he was.

And there I was with him in an apartment in town for our honeymoon. The honeymoon was short and there was nothing much to do. Everyone had been advised to stay home. All we had was Netflix and Amazon Prime. We watched shows, ate, and had sex. Was I deeply happy? I wasn't sure. *It is what it is*, I thought.

After the honeymoon, we went back to Mum's house. Due to COVID, all our plans had been turned around. We had a discussion about staying at Mum's. We could save some money if we stayed. We had our room (my old room) and our own space; it was perfect, and I didn't mind.

He was there right beside me, but there was nothing – no joy and no happiness. Spending time with me was like something he had to get done, and then he could resume being on his phone. It's funny how quickly things changed – the spark, the love, everything; it went away so quickly, quicker than a butterfly flapping its wings. At one time he would spend all day with me, telling me how amazing I was and how much he loved me. I never saw his phone once, but now that we were married, he no longer expressed his love, and his phone? Well, that was all I saw.

I raised it several times: 'Please, can you just put your phone down?' I would ask. I noticed that, in the middle of the night, he would wake up to charge his phone. That's when I knew it was serious. He was married to his phone, and that would, of course, cause problems, and we argued about it.

I turned over in bed to see what he was up to, what he was doing, and he was on Facebook, scrolling, looking at a woman. I watched as he scrolled down and then scrolled back up to look at the previous picture. I watched as he zoomed in on her face. I didn't know what else to do but speak up. 'Who is she?' I asked.

'Oh, she's a Nigerian actor,' he replied. *Okay*, I thought. Did that make it okay if she was a celebrity? I wasn't sure. It still didn't seem right. I noticed this happening on a few occasions. I would see him looking at a female on his phone, analysing the picture, but I never asked again. It would have seemed strange that I was looking. I felt hopeless, but it wasn't the phone I had the problem with – everyone uses their phones, and so do I – it was the consistency. I never saw him use his phone that much before marriage. In fact, the only time I saw his phone was when he called his mum or brothers in Nigeria. He would bring it out, an old Samsung, call them, and put it back into his pocket.

'Why couldn't you just be honest with me in courtship and show me the real you?' I asked. I'm an open and honest person. I say things as they are, and I wanted to with him. He was my husband, and I should be able to, but it was a dead end. He never listened to what I was saying. *Had he heard me?* I wondered on numerous occasions. *Had he heard what I just said?*

It was hard. The lockdown meant we couldn't go out, so we were stuck together for what felt like forever. Being indoors and together all day wasn't bad, but the energy between us was different. After showering, I would put on some makeup, just a small amount, to look or feel better. I tried hard for him to notice me once again, to tell me I was beautiful, to tell me how amazing he thought I was, but there was no recognition. There was no 'You're beautiful.' There were no sweet words. At a point,

I felt as if we were just roommates. One month turned into two months, and I was confused as to how I had even got there. Where had I been? What on earth had happened? Although I was in a place I had called home for so many years, I was confused as to where I really was in life. How had my life changed like that? Oh, dear, I was confused. I was lost. Physically, I was standing straight yet mentally, I was bewildered.

This was God's will for my life, right? Let me run with it, I continued, and I prayed for peace, for a good marriage, that I would be happy, and that he would treat me as if I were special once again.

Initially, when we had married, he'd made comments about my being pregnant. 'I know what I put inside you,' he would say on so many occasions.

Unfortunately, I didn't get pregnant, and my period kept coming.

It was evening, 7 p.m., and he sat me down. He said that he had something to tell me, that he believed it was the right time.

I wondered what was going on. I was nervous. What did he want to say? I said, 'Okay,' and I listened.

He told me about a woman he knew before me.

Okay, I thought.

'Well, she got pregnant.'

'Do you have a child?' I asked, my heart beating fast. Where was this conversation going?

'No, she had an abortion.'

I didn't understand what he was telling me. 'Why are you telling me now?' I asked.

He explained that he thought it was the best time for me to know. It was only a few days later when I realised he had told me, so I knew he didn't have a problem, and he could get a woman pregnant, and if I didn't have a baby, it wasn't his fault. At the time, I was upset that I hadn't known it before.

'Why didn't you tell me this in courtship when we were telling each other everything?' I said, upset.

During courtship, he had drawn me in by acting vulnerable and emotionally open. 'You know everything about me, Jasmine, you know everything,' he would say. Clearly, he kept some information on hold, and this was one of the many revelations he made to me during our marriage. I wondered why I hadn't thought about it deeply enough. I didn't ask about his past or his previous relationships. What had happened? Were they in a similar situation I was in? Did he treat them badly too?

'Why are you upset? It should be me that's upset. This happened to me. I lost the baby.' He had reversed the role of victim, making me out to be the abuser whilst he himself was the victim. It was the beginning of a behaviour I understood later, playing the victim when not the victim and projection. He accused me of hurting him when, in fact, he had hurt me; this was projection. I was upset, and of course, he was upset. We faced different directions that night.

Walking in the beautiful green commons behind our house, I prayed that I would just be pregnant so I could make him happy, and maybe things would be better, and he would treat me better, maybe he would recognise me once again. Perhaps the happiness would come when we had our child. I prayed, I prayed, I prayed. I walked around the park seven times over, praying that God would place a beautiful seed in my womb.

As we sat in the room in the early evening with nothing to do, I wanted some answers. 'What, exactly, do you want from the marriage? What do you want me to be like?' I asked, wondering if I was going about it all wrong. Maybe he just wanted me to cook and serve him food. I had no idea.

'Nothing. This is fine. Marriage is simple. It doesn't take too much work,' he would say.

When he said that marriage didn't take much work, I knew something wasn't right. I knew he really didn't understand how things worked. I had never been married before, but I knew it took work. I knew because of how lost, lonely, and sad I felt. If no work was put into it, I would find myself in another man's arms, and that was the sad truth.

I continued to pray, trusting, leaning on the all-sufficient God, the God that could do the impossible and make the marriage a happy one for me. I understand now what they mean when they say that you should marry your best friend. If we had been best friends, maybe the times we were bored and had nothing to do would have been more fun. Maybe we would have connected with happiness and real, authentic love between us. It was only later, I realised that unfortunate situations can still happen with high school sweethearts. The love can fizzle. The interests can change. Marriage is so powerful, and it is extremely life-changing. It takes work, and the work needs to be from both parties. If no work is put in, a marriage between even the best of friends will fail. I will not dive into giving marriage advice because I'm not the one to give it, but I do know, for a fact, that when both parties work together, are honest with each other, are real, oh, so real, then it will work. When there are lies, distrust, and bad communication, then that marriage needs work, serious work, or else it will fail.

The boredom at home, sitting in silence, wondering, thinking about what he might be up to, and what he was doing was getting to be too much. I was beginning to lose my peace, and I needed to find a distraction. I decided to enrol on an online course to keep me busy and keep my mind occupied in another way. I had always wanted to attend Bible college, so I decided to look for a course on Christianity.

I managed to find one. It was called 'The Foundation of Christianity'. I was happy, and I enrolled. Whilst I did my course for one hour each day, he sat there on the other side of the bed, on his phone, with his earphones in. I will admit that I was never at peace. After one hour of studying and with nothing truly changing, I realised that I needed something more. I needed another distraction, one that would truly take me away from reality. I looked for a good TV show, the type of TV show you watch and forget what time of day it is. I looked for a show that would distract me from the life that I had locked myself into, a show that would make me experience another reality, another dimension, a series packed with the characters' dilemmas – that's what I wanted.

Scrolling on Amazon Prime, I found one. It helped, but it wasn't good enough to make me forget where I was and what my new life was. Of course, the truth was that I was married to him, and I had to accept it. There was no running away from reality. It was still so hard. We were both in the same room, in the same bed, with me sitting upright on one side of the bed and him lying down on the other side. We were close but so far apart.

His outward behaviour and appearance were very humble. He looked innocent, and he didn't give away his abusive personality, and it had me somewhat confused.

People would call him, asking how we were doing. 'Yes, we are good. We thank God. We are enjoying ourselves, still in our honeymoon phase,' he would respond every time.

Whilst I sat and listened, I wondered if he actually believed what he was saying. Did he genuinely believe this was good? Was he happy and enjoying this, the no communication, the silence, the arguments, the awkwardness – was it good? Believe me, whenever he answered phone calls and gave that response, I was perplexed. I even doubted myself. My mind always raced with questions. *Was it good, Jas? Was it actually good?* I wondered.

I wondered how he could just lay down all day and do nothing to better himself, nothing to build himself up, and nothing to learn.

'Why not do an online course, too?' I asked.

He responded, 'Okay, I will.' We searched online together for a course for him to do. He wanted to do computer science, which was also what he did at university.

Together, we found something suitable and he registered for the course.

He started it for the first two or three days, but then I realised he wasn't doing it as much any more. He eventually said that it wasn't something he wanted to do, that he had already studied it at university, and that was the end of the online course discussion.

'You should do something to build yourself up,' I said; I couldn't stand to watch him do nothing day after day and week after week. I am a go-getter. I am somebody who likes to go above and beyond, making sure I get the most I can get out of a situation. Whenever I have free time, I see that I use it effectively, and now we had a lot of free time due to the lockdown, and I wanted to make the most of it. I wanted us both to make the most of it.

He was different. He enjoyed doing nothing. I didn't understand it.

'I told you before marriage: I like to sleep and watch football or play chess on my phone,' he said. I didn't remember that conversation. *When did he tell me this?* I wondered. He was really content with how things were, and I wasn't. It felt as though we were on different pages of two different books.

I sought advice as to what to do. I asked my sister.

'Just get on with things, and he will eventually join you,' she said.

I did, and he didn't. He was content and fine with the situation. Again, I was perplexed.

The shower was time I could get away and just be free. I would stay in the shower for 30 minutes, crying out to God, praying for an escape, praying for the marriage, praying for my husband to change and to love me once again. I put on music, so if I cried, no one would hear. I sat on the bathroom floor with the shower on, the water running down my body, the hot water allowing me to experience a feeling other than what I felt the remaining 23.5 hours of the day. When I had been in the shower long enough, I feared coming out and having to go back into the bedroom.

I always found it so awkward. Would he say something? Would I? What would he be doing? Would I tell him to shower, too? Maybe I was overthinking. My mind always raced with thoughts, and I could hardly keep up.

'Uh, Jas? Come on. Get out of the shower,' I would tell myself. I spent as long as I could in the bathroom, creaming my body, maybe putting on a small amount of makeup, again, in the hope of being told I was beautiful. Finally, I needed clothes, and I needed to go back into the bedroom. I had to. I couldn't stay in the bathroom forever. Every day, it was the same feeling, the same emotion, the same feeling of dread.

I decided to start looking for a job, working from home. I made a few applications and waited for the outcome. The good news came, a door opened, and I got a job. It was a job working from home for the government. I was excited. Finally, I would not be stuck, asking him what he wanted to do with me. I could get on and do my own thing, and we could meet again once I'd finished.

I have always been a hardworking girl, putting my all into everything I do. At university, I studied exceptionally hard. I went to the library, day and night, to make sure I secured a position at the top of the class. On the weekends, I drove a total of nine hours to get to church on Friday night and Sunday morning.

Honestly, I was a serious girl with my head screwed on the right way, or so I thought. I always looked for new ways to build myself up and grow, learning something new, like a new skill or experience.

'I'm going to write goals today,' I told him in excitement. 'Do you want to write some with me?'

'I don't believe in goals,' he responded. 'People write down goals and start stressing to achieve them. I don't want to stress,' he continued. I couldn't believe what I was hearing. We were so, so different. We had nothing in common. Why did none of this show in courtship? He had really wrapped himself up in a golden package for me, only for me to realise that it had never been gold but copper all along. His true colours were now showing. He wasn't bad, I thought, but he was not for me. We were not a good match at all. Nevertheless, I wondered if it was my duty to encourage him and change him. I wondered if that was why God had put us together. I didn't know, but all I could do was try to encourage myself.

I thought that my working would motivate him, but it didn't. From there, I didn't know what else to do. I just had to continue doing me, I would tell myself.

'We don't do Bible study together? We don't do anything together. You are always on your phone. You don't even come for walks with me.' The arguments continued. All I wanted was a companion, a friend, someone with whom to work and talk, to share visions and goals with the friend I had during courtship.

'I told you: I like sleeping, and it's too cold to go on walks,' he responded. The more he showed me this character, the more I grew distant from him.

A few days earlier, I had received the equipment for my job. The atmosphere between us was dark and gloomy. We had just been arguing about not doing anything together.

'I want us to go and celebrate,' he said.

'That'd be great,' I responded.

'Let's go for a walk, have a picnic, have some wine – non-alcoholic wine, of course – and do Bible study,' he said.

'Wow! I'd love that. Let's go.' Although we had been arguing, I was happy he was not emotional, and he wanted to celebrate that moment with me. I was happy; I was really happy.

We walked in silence with nothing to say. That was how our walks were, sometimes. Other times, he would tell me about his friends and his life in Nigeria, which, I must admit, although I love Nigerian movies and the culture, I never found interesting. Nevertheless, at least we were talking, and I never complained. I would listen, saying words like 'Really,' or 'Wow,' occasionally, and the conversation continued. It was mainly one-sided, but I was happy. At least we were together, and he wasn't on his phone.

On that occasion, maybe because we had been arguing, we didn't speak. We walked in silence until we finally got to the commons' second park, the one with the beautiful lake, and we found a spot to sit under the shade. We brought the blanket, wine, and Bible out of the bag and sat down. I didn't say anything first – I wanted to let him start; I was excited.

'I just want to tell you how you hurt me,' he said.

What? I was shocked he'd started with that. I was also shocked by what he'd said.

The argument began. People walked past, probably thinking that we were a lovely couple having a date; wine, wine glasses, and the Bible – how romantic. People walking past smiled – if only they knew.

'Why did you say we were going to celebrate my getting a new job when you just wanted to tell me how I'd offended you or what I did wrong? What is the point?' I said, wanting to cry.

'Jasmine, you should listen and understand me,' he said.

'Yes, I do, but we came out to celebrate. We were supposed to do Bible study like you said.'

'We can't always do Bible study. Is that all married couples do?' he responded.

Oh, my gosh – he was driving me crazy. He brought me out, telling me we were going to do Bible study and now he was complaining. *What was the actual point, Jas? What was the point?*

I stood and said I was going back home. I walked for a bit, and he called me back. Of course, I went back.

'I thought we were here to have a good time. Can we celebrate me getting a job and move forward?' I asked exhaustingly with tears rolling down my eyes.

'Yes, but I really need you to know why I was not happy so we can resolve this.'

I realised at that moment that if I tried to address anything in good faith, he was not satisfied nor fulfilled until he had the upper hand. He had to have control. I was starting to become familiar with the pattern. He would confuse and distract me until I became so overwhelmed by what's been thrown at me then, at that point, he would make peace.

He continued so I stood up and left again. Now, he followed me, pulled me back and said I should stay. I was crying my eyes out. I was so hurt. It was not a good celebration anymore, and unfortunately, it was the first of many unhappy, sad celebrations.

The argument continued. I picked myself up and left him to celebrate by himself. That was the beginning of my leaving him. It's true when they say that a woman leaves mentally before she leaves physically. I had been leaving him mentally, unknowingly. That was two months into the marriage in May 2020.

My walking away was another argument. He couldn't get over that I'd walked away from him, leaving him alone in the park. He told me that he felt embarrassed and lonely. I couldn't get over that he'd taken me to the park to argue. Arguments with him were exceptionally confusing. I lost track on many occasions, but he never did. He would change the topic, oh so slightly, to something not related to the original conversation, usually to something I had done wrong previously. I'd often find myself in defensive mode as he brought up a situation or issue that had a kernel of truth, but that's not all. When I attempted to defend myself, he claimed my defence was an accusation. Taking my focus off what he had done and focusing on my mistake led to my defending myself again.

By twisting my words and misrepresenting my motives, thoughts, and feelings, he was redefining my reality, and I didn't even know it. My thoughts were everywhere, and I was being accused of distorted thinking and not making sense. He would bring up red herrings, which led to the conversation quickly diverting in another heated direction. Expressing my feelings was hard, and I was scared that if I expressed my feelings, we would argue, and I would be left to feel hurt and down.

Very often, he put words into my mouth: 'You think I don't have emotions? Are you the only one with feelings?' It was a downward spiral. The only crime I had committed was simply to express my feelings, and I was suffering the penalty for it; I suffered in my mind.

It was horrible, and I had literally had enough of his behaviour, but what could I do? We were married, joined together; he was my husband. I was not attracted to him at all. He was not who I thought he was, and the man I was getting to know was the cause of more tears than smiles of happiness.

The arguments continued, and I was completely fed up. On one occasion, I took my rings off out of anger and chucked them at him. I was done. That was just over two months into the marriage, and I was done. We did not suffer from first-year marriage problems – this was something a lot deeper, a more serious issue, a hidden abuse that no one could identify, not even me at the time. It was so subtle and unassuming; it was hard to pinpoint. Some people think that abuse is always physical, an abuse that causes bruises and scars, but this abuse, this was an abuse that ate away at my mind, an abuse that made me question the very essence of who I was. It was an abuse that later pushed me into A&E.

After the argument, Nick called Pastor Daniel. It was an action he took regularly as time went on. He would make jokes and explain that he feared me, that I was abusive and scary.

With my mind constantly racing, trying to make sense of what life had become and how I would survive, I often felt trapped, not knowing who I could speak to that could help me. Nick explained to Pastor Daniel that I had taken off my rings and thrown them at him.

Pastor Daniel came round that evening to help resolve the problem. He explained to us the situation of a woman who had taken off her rings and had thrown them at her husband. He explained how the rings had hit the husband's eye, and his eye started bleeding. The husband then left the wife and has since remarried a beautiful woman with whom he has two children. The previous wife was, however, left alone and single.

Nick and I sat, listening to the story. I understood the message that was being said. I understood that I was the wife in the story. The 'crazy wife'. Pastor Daniel said that we had done the same thing; however, I was fortunate in my situation in that it hadn't hit his eye, that he was still there, and had no reason to leave me. I wondered what Nick thought as he listened to the story.

I felt awkward. I felt as though I was in the wrong for what I had done. If the rings had hit Nick's eye, then I, like the woman in the story, would be left all alone and single forever. It felt as though I had not been heard, and the reason behind my throwing the rings was irrelevant. The real issue had been brushed over, and my actions were the real cause for concern. I didn't like the story, but all in all, we made up, and I put the rings back on. But mentally, I was not okay.

I continued working every day. I worked in the spare room upstairs whilst he stayed downstairs in our room all day. He was still furloughed, so he had nothing to do. When I finished working and came into the room, he was lying down and on his phone. I always wondered, what he'd been doing all day.

Chapter 6

It Will Get Better

'I'm pregnant!' I said to myself, delighted.

I was overwhelmed; a little human was growing inside of me. I knew Nick would be happy. He wanted a baby from the very start of marriage. *Finally*, I thought.

It was his birthday coming up and I had booked us to stay in an apartment down south near the beach. I wanted to surprise him, I wanted to make the moment I tell him about my pregnancy special, so I waited. It was one week to his birthday so I thought I'd order him a little gift that implies he will soon be a dad for his birthday present. I found a card that said *Happy Birthday Daddy!* I thought it was sweet. I also saw a mug that said *You are going to be a daddy!* Perfect! I would just hand him the presents, let him open it and see his reaction!! I was excited about this plan.

One week to keep the news to myself was hard. I was so excited and wanted to share with someone. I told my mum and Jacklyn. They were thrilled. Jacklyn was excited to be an aunty, mum was happy to have another grandchild, making her a grandmother of four. I explained how I was going to share the news with Nick. They said it was a really nice idea, and Nick will be so happy. Jacklyn joked that she wanted a card and present too, stating that she will be an aunty. It was a great moment.

When he wasn't around, I wrapped up the present neatly and wrote a nice message in the card. As much as Nick had surprised me with his behaviour after we got married and had left me crying more than I had during any other period in my life, I always made the effort. He was my husband, and this was another opportunity to bring us closer together; another opportunity for him to love me again and treat me well.

Surely now I am pregnant, he will treat me with love and care and he would not want to see me cry, sad or depressed, I thought.

It was Saturday, his birthday, and we started our drive down south. It was a two-hour drive; it was far but I knew it was worth it. Five minutes into the drive his phone rang. It was his family. They'd joined him to a WhatsApp call in which he stayed on the phone for 1 hour and 50 minutes. Initially, it was sweet. They were wishing him happy birthday and sang him a song. I loved the vibrant vibe and connection he had with his family. After some time though, they were discussing some family affairs in Nigeria where one of his brothers wanted to buy land. There were several occasions he could have come off the phone, but he stayed listening and chipping in wherever he could. I mean I don't know whether I was being selfish, but this was time for us to spend together. It was supposed to be a nice road trip with us talking, laughing and listening to music. This is how it usually was; I mean before marriage of course. We would go on road trips, long drives and have so much fun on the way. However, I should have known things had changed. We were married now and he didn't know I was pregnant yet. Can I blame him? As he chatted away, I felt sad. Where had the romance and love gone? It was just three months into marriage and I felt like all my energy had been sucked away and I could no longer be the happy person I used to be. As he was on the phone, the music on the radio was low…practically off. I decided to increase it. I needed something other than his voice and my thoughts to listen to. I increased it loud enough to hear but also at a level which he could still continue his conversation. When I increased it, he looked at me, then looked away and continued his conversation. I cried a few times in the car. He hadn't known of course. They were the silent tears; as the tears trickled down my face I wiped them off.

When we had got close to the destination, I was struggling to find which road to turn onto. Making wrong turns and getting frustrated, I thought he would help me. *If only he would help me.*

'Nick, I need some help,' I said.

He apologised to his family and said he had to go.

'Do you know where we are? Are we here?' he asked.

'No, I'm not sure which turn, and you spent the whole drive on the phone!!' I responded abruptly.

'I'm sorry,' he said as he looked intently on the satnav.

Finally, we found the destination. I parked, and we went inside. He could tell I was not happy and apologised, explaining that he should have come off the phone. He then took hold of my hands and said I looked beautiful today. I smiled. It was the first time he had said this in a while. I don't remember the last time he had complimented me. He was making me feel special once again.

We went for a walk, and I decided to surprise him with the present when we got back after we had lunch. Lunch was delicious. Nick had prepared it for the both of us before we left in the morning. I appreciated Nick for cooking and preparing one of my favourite foods. It was a Nigerian dish – yam porridge.

After eating, I decided to give him his present. He opened the mug, said 'thank you' and put it down. He clearly hadn't read it. I guess he was probably wondering why I had got him a mug for his birthday. He then began to open the card, but I wanted him to read the mug so I asked him to look back at the mug. He picked it up, read it and paused. He looked at me then looked back at the mug. At this point, I was wondering what was going on in his head. He didn't say anything. He was shocked, I guess. Or maybe he didn't understand. I mean the mug said, *You are going to be a daddy.* It was simple, right?

What felt like 50 seconds later, he smiled and fell onto the bed. I smiled. Getting back up and reading the card, he looked at me and said, 'Are you serious?'

'Yes!' I responded, excitedly. He then gave me a hug. He was filled with joy and so was I. It was a special moment. I was so excited for the start of something new. He wanted to share the news with Pastor Daniel which I said was fine. He called Pastor Daniel, who didn't answer. Then he called Pastor Kenny. After sharing the news, Pastor Kenny congratulated us and prayed for us. She was excited and said she would tell Pastor Daniel. Afterwards, he said we should tell my mum. He obviously hadn't known I had previously told her. 'Oh, she knows already. I've told her because I couldn't keep it to myself,' I said. He responded with, 'Oh.' Despite this, the celebration continued. We laughed and talked about the fact we were going to be parents. I thought the surprise had gone well. However, I hadn't known that this would later be used against me. The fact that I had not told him first was going to be a massive deal. Two days later, when we got back home, he let me know in no uncertain terms that he was not happy he was not the first person to find out.

'You told your mum and Jacklyn, and me last!' he said.

'It's only because I wanted to surprise you. I wanted to tell you on your birthday. I wanted it to be a special moment,' I said with a smile on my face.

'No, you should have told me first. We decide together who we will tell,' he snapped.

'Okay, I'm sorry. I found out I was pregnant on Saturday and it was still a week to your birthday. I wanted it to be special for us,' I said.

'You talk about us working together, but you keep important news from me,' he responded.

I reminisced at the moment I knew I was pregnant. How happy I was. How happy I thought Nick would be and how he would now make me feel special. I reminisced at the hours I spent searching for a gift and card to make his birthday memorable. I reminisced about when I had told Jacklyn and my mum and explained to them what I had planned. I remembered their reaction. How they thought it was sweet and how happy Nick would be. I reminisced on the drive when he was on the phone the entire time. I reminisced on the time he opened the presents and then his reaction when I told him I had told Mum. My mind was taking me back to everything. I had thought it went well and everything was okay. He had thought the opposite. I couldn't believe it.

'Nick, I just wanted to surprise you!' I now said out of annoyance. 'I wanted to make your birthday special by telling you the amazing news on your birthday.'

'…yet you told your mum and Jacklyn. Does that make sense?' he said.

'Okay Nick. I'm sorry but I had to tell mum and Jacklyn. I was so excited and I couldn't keep it in.'

'You should have told me. It doesn't make sense. This is news you should tell your husband first,' he said.

I started to cry. All my thinking that our relationship would now be different was a dream yet to come true. As I cried, he huffed and looked away.

'Why are you crying? You should have just told me first…this is your fault. If you had told me first, we wouldn't be here right now,' he said.

I continued to cry. I was speechless and so deeply sad. *Nothing is ever good enough*, I thought *and clearly this mistake I had made, was not an easy one to forgive.*

The more I explained that I had wanted to surprise him, the more he continued to say the same thing that he should have known first.

We were going round in circles. How many times would I explain that it was a surprise, and I was sorry? He was not happy for the entire day. It lasted three or four days, in fact, seven days later, we were sat in Pastor Daniel's office whilst Nick explained what I had done.

Whilst I sat there, I wondered if Pastor Daniel would tell me that I was wrong to. I didn't know what to expect. Everything was taking me by surprise. I had tears in my ears as I listened to Nick explain my wrongdoing. Pastor Daniel surprised me. He told Nick that it was okay and explained that I only wanted to make it special for him. It was at that moment, that Nick looked at me and said, 'Okay, I have forgiven you.' Pastor Daniel was happy and told us to hug each other, which we did, awkwardly. Pastor Daniel asked if I was happy. I responded, 'Yes.' I wondered whether he saw that something was not right. I'm not sure. He prayed for us and then we left.

It was draining, expressing myself repeatedly only to not be heard. Although Nick had apologised, I had emotionally suffered the consequences of my actions. It wasn't so easy to forget what had happened.

Pastor Daniel hadn't said anything different to what I had said. I wondered why he couldn't just listen to me in the first place and understand where I was coming from but at least it had now come to an end and he had forgiven me. *It will get better Jas. It will*, I told myself.

Chapter 7

Something Else

22nd June 2020, three months into our marriage, we were on our way to the first scan. It should have been a time of great joy and happiness; rather, we argued. We argued on the journey going there and on the way home. That morning, we were running late, and I was anxious. He doesn't drive, so I calculated the time, planned the journey, tried to get ready quickly, concerned about him getting ready, too. I had worked for an hour in the morning. He wasn't working and had been waiting for me. We had planned for him to get ready in the morning whilst I worked; then, once I'd finished, I would get ready quickly, and we would leave.

I went downstairs to get ready, only to notice that he wasn't ready at all. He was still in pyjamas, waiting for me. That's when the argument started. 'I thought you would have been ready, so once I was ready, we could quickly go,' I said.

'I'll shower quickly now,' he responded.

I was stressed, thinking about getting there in time and finding parking. Not only was my mind filled with things to do that needed to get done, but I also wondered what the scan would be like. It was an internal scan, where they put the scanner into your vagina, and I was nervous. I had so many things on my mind, and somehow, so did he. It felt like we were both pregnant. It was like two pregnant sisters living together, both trying to express their emotions.

I lay on the bed in the spare room upstairs, the room in which I'd worked. I lay there, looking at the picture of our scan. My mind, my thoughts, were everywhere. I was pregnant with his child – why was he treating me like that?

When he came upstairs to join me, the disagreement continued: 'The Bible says he who finds a wife finds a good thing and receives favour from the Lord – where is the good thing?' he asked me. I couldn't believe my ears. It hurt so much – how could he say such a horrible thing? Even if you thought something like that, you didn't need to say it. The abuse came in a calculated and purposeful way. He knew just how to upset me, and it worked every single time.

'How can you say that? Get out!' I shouted. Anger, rage and adrenaline filled my body. I was angry. He certainly knew how to wind me up. I shouted, I screamed, I cried. The same man who used to compliment me and shower me with attention and love now devalued and degraded me. This affected me more than I knew.

I cried all night, and I cried myself to sleep. 'Lord, help me. Please, help me and help my baby. Let my baby not feel what I feel.'

I slept upstairs that night; he stayed downstairs in our bedroom.

The second scan was the same. We were not on good terms for a reason I cannot remember. The atmosphere between us was awkward as usual. On the drive, he had his headphones in and was watching something on his phone. The radio was on and I listened to LBC. We didn't say anything to each other. We were on time for the appointment but the car park was full and finding parking was becoming impossible. I was getting stressed while he sat there not saying anything. Due to the lockdown, only I could go in for the scan. *Thank God* I thought. I liked going in by myself. I couldn't imagine the both of us in there together.

After I finally found parking, I was frustrated as I was now running late and I didn't know my way around the hospital. *Where am I going?* I thought, as I looked down to see the name of the ward on the letter. I left the car, closed the door and didn't say a word. I guess I knew he wouldn't be happy about that, but we hadn't talked all morning, what was the difference now? I was tired of trying my best to be validated and approved, only to be left emotionally drained. Better to just keep quiet, right?

Walking inside the scan room, I felt peace. I was excited to see my little baby. I didn't know who I was seeing. I didn't know whether it was a midwife or doctor. Nothing had been clear, but I was still at peace, nevertheless. The scan was relaxing, I sat on the hospital bed whilst the doctor put a cold jelly like gel on my stomach and rubbed a handheld device called a transducer over my belly. As the doctor moved the transducer around, I looked at the TV in front of me whilst the doctor pointed out baby's legs and arms. He asked if I wanted to know the sex of the baby. Of course, I did!!

'Yes!!' I responded.

I couldn't have been happier. It didn't feel real. It felt like a dream. The doctor told me I was having a boy. I was thrilled. Deep down, I always wanted a boy. I was smiling so much; I just couldn't stop. I felt alive, full of energy, and at peace. When the scan had finished and I walked back to the car, the nervous anxious feeling came back. I wondered whether he would tell me off for not saying 'bye' when I left. I wondered if he was in a good or bad mood. *It would be better for me to wait and see his mood before talking* I thought. Surely he will be excited to know how the scan went? I had no idea. Nothing was predictable any more. As I walked towards the car, it felt like my muscles were tensing and my heart rate increased rapidly. I felt nervous and anxious.

I got into the car and didn't say anything. I didn't have the strength to argue. I tried my best to remember the feeling I had in the scan room. I pictured myself lying on the hospital bed. I was trying to escape reality and relive the short-lived feeling I had in the hospital the best I could. I gave him the papers the doctors had given me, along with the picture of the scan. We drove silently back home. When we got home, it started. 'You did not share anything with me about the scan. Do you know how that makes me feel?' he said.

'You never asked,' I responded. I believe my pregnancy made me somewhat strong to put up with his remarks, however, I was still weak and entering into an argument with him would affect me more than I thought.

'You are the reason communication is bad in this marriage!' he said.

The argument continued, leaving me angry and exhausted. Him continuously blaming me for actions or behaviours was hurtful as I had tried on so many occasions to make it work. I tried to make us a team.

'I fear being pregnant with you again,' I said to him. This was the first time I'd said it, however, I said it on many more occasions. Although I was still pregnant with our son, I couldn't imagine going through it again another two or three times, the emotional rollercoaster of moments of highs and moments of lows. I needed a plan. I planned the next pregnancy in my head, hoping that life would be better and I would have more money to treat myself to nice spa treatments and hotels so I could at least make myself happy.

I explained to him that when I'm pregnant again with his next baby, I would book myself into hotels for a few days so we wouldn't argue. He shrugged and laughed, not really paying any attention to what I was saying, not paying any attention to the altitude, depth, or the actual meaning behind my words. His pregnant wife was crying out for help. Pregnancy was supposed to be an enjoyable time, where I was happy and being treated like a queen, being treated with care as the baby grew inside my womb. Rather, I cried every day, and my mental health was deteriorating.

Oh, how I feared pregnancy with him again. I looked online, searching how arguing affects the baby in the womb. Did my baby feel my emotions? Did he feel when I cried? Did he cry with me? The results always made me sad. I was upset that it could affect my little baby, that he could feel his mum's tears, that he could feel the unhappiness, the emotion. I was upset, but I tried to stay strong, 'I'll be strong for you, little baby,' I said to him whilst holding my stomach.

I found an article online about the effect arguing has on Mummy and baby, and I showed it to my husband, explaining that this was having a bad effect on me. I pleaded to him asking if he could please treat me better and stop arguing with me. 'Please, treat me better because everything affects our baby,' I said, pleading for help.

Again, he didn't take what I'd said seriously. He never listened to my words, and the arguments continued.

I noticed he always watched *The Maury Show*, with women talking about their problems with their spouses or husbands. 'You always watch women talk about their problems in their relationships, but you don't even deal with the issues in yours,' I said. 'Maybe I should go on the show so you can hear me,' I shouted.

It was ridiculous to be so concerned about women sharing their problems with their spouses but missing the same things when it came to the woman in his life, not seeing what was wrong. Knowing it would never happen, I wondered what it would be like if I went on the show. I wondered what his reaction would be, seeing his wife there. I also wondered if another woman on the show had expressed the same issues I'd faced – would he sympathise with her? Would he still enjoy watching the show? Would he finally realise there was an issue in the marriage that was not being dealt with?

I was in my first trimester, and I felt all of the symptoms of pregnancy. It was terrible: the nausea, drowsiness, and exhaustion. After a heated discussion, I cried myself to sleep in the spare room again. That time, whilst crying myself to sleep, I made sure I had a bucket near me so when I needed it, I could vomit without having to go downstairs. I put the Bible on my phone to listen to whilst I cried. I cried so much it hurt, and my eyes were red and burning with pain.

Waking up in the morning, I prayed for God to give me the strength to work that day and for Him to help me.

We exchanged words. My voice was always louder than his. He was loud enough for me to hear but quiet, so no one else in the house heard. After the argument got to be too much, I would be so angry that I would scream. My mum would come into the room, confused as to what was going on with her pregnant daughter who was full of tears and rage whilst her son-in-law was calm and collected.

'I don't know, Ma – I am just trying to help her,' he would say, placing his hands one on top of the other. Ugh! It made me feel sick every time he said that. Every single argument, when my mum got involved, he would reply the same way: 'I don't know what's wrong with her. I just want to help her.' I could not grasp how he was trying to help me whenever we argued, and he said things to bring me down. My head, my mind, my body, flooded with adrenaline. What was going on? I was confused. My mind was chaotic and unstable. I struggled, and because I was never truly heard, I suffered in silence.

I no longer felt safe at home. The very place that should have been my safe space had turned into a ball of fire. It felt as if I was playing with fire, playing in the fire, sleeping in the fire, and eating in the fire every day. After patronising and minimising my feelings, he acted shocked and surprised with my response whilst expressing loving concern at my 'instability'.

He often attempted to convince me that his behaviour was accidental or it hadn't happened in the first place. He pretended he didn't understand things, and he often would say, 'I've never done this before,' as an excuse for his subtle emotional abuse.

'I've not been in this situation before,' he would say to me during my pregnancy. He would explain he had never been married before and had a pregnant wife. It didn't make sense. I had never been married or pregnant either, but I was getting through it. I was experiencing things I had not experienced before – the symptoms of pregnancy, changes in my body, heartburn, chest and back pain – I experienced it all, yet I was making it through. I kept on going; it was all I could do.

The third scan was the same as the first two. Something needed to be done, I thought. 'I think Mum should follow us to every scan going forward so we won't argue,' I said.

He agreed.

We made the arrangements with Mum so she could drop us off. It worked. The arguments stopped when we went for the scans, and we started having happy hospital visits. It felt good, walking through the hospital doors, holding hands, excited that we would soon have a baby. He would sit in the waiting room, holding my bag and jacket whilst I was lying on the hospital bed in the scan room, feeling excited to go back out and share the exciting news with him about how baby is getting on. *Finally*, I thought. *Finally*.

In the good times, I often told myself that the abuse really wasn't that bad. I spoke myself into being better; to not get emotional or angry easily, to treat him nicely, making sure I take time to think about what I want to say before I say it. I told myself to stay silent unless it's important, responding only when spoken to. I told myself to be my best self for him and work on myself continually.

Somehow that would help, that would make everything better.

Chapter 8

The Hidden Actions

I walked out of the house, upset. I was exhausted fighting a fight I couldn't win. There was no more strength to continue and no more endorphins to keep me settled. I was four months pregnant and was struggling to manage with the emotional turmoil ride I was on. I knew he had been watching pornography because I had seen it in his history.

I started to realise that when I walked into the room, he would turn his phone face down, go onto the main screen or lock the screen then look at me to see what I wanted. I started to wonder what he was up to; it was as if he was hiding something. One thing with Nick was he always left his phone around when he wasn't using it. If he was going to the toilet or downstairs, he would leave it in the room. On one occasion, I couldn't help myself. I picked it up to see what he was up to. When I unlocked his phone, I checked his internet history. I don't know why I had checked this. When I opened his history, I saw a porn website. I was completely shocked. I guess I knew he was up to something but realising that it was in fact true was hard. It felt as if every day there was a new obstacle to face and attempt to overcome. I knew if I spoke to him about it, he would want to know why I had checked his phone. An issue would come up about me not trusting him. I would be blamed for my actions and the situation would leave me feeling belittled, especially as Pastor Daniel had very often said during his preaching that a woman should not check her husband's phone, which I never really understood. Thoughts were racing in my mind. What do I do? How do I approach this?

God, what do I do? I said inside.

I heard his footsteps and quickly put the phone down. *Do not make any mistake now*, I thought. I needed a plan before I confronted him about it.

When he was back in the room on his phone, I couldn't think clearly. I now had many thoughts. Was he watching it right there…in front of me? He was sat at the opposite end of the bed so I couldn't see what he was doing. With all the thoughts racing in my mind, I decided to leave the house, go for a walk and call a deaconess at my church. *Let me get some godly advise*, I thought.

'I know I shouldn't have checked his phone, but I did,' I said to her as I explained what I'd seen.

'Yes, you shouldn't have,' she responded. She then gave me the godly advice I had called for.

'You need to pray for him,' she said.

She suggested I raise it with him but not to tell him I'd checked his phone.

'Just ask him if he watches it. He may be honest,' she said.

I thought it was a good idea, I wanted a marriage where we can talk freely to each other about things, no matter what it was. We had been on the phone for an hour as I walked up and down the park behind my house. I had cried a few times on the phone as the thought of him watching pornography left me feeling ugly, unwanted and unworthy. She comforted me and she said I should be strong for Baby. It started to get dark, cold, and my back began to hurt. I had to go back home. Whilst walking home, I was encouraged to speak to him about it. It went against my plan of being silent and not raising issues but I couldn't help it. Truly, I could not let it eat me up inside. If I raise it then at least I have done something.

When I got into the room, the tension between us was weird, as always. I'm not sure why.

'Hey,' I said.

'Hey,' he responded.

'What are you up to?' I asked.

'Nothing. Just waiting for you to come back,' he replied as he put his phone down, smiling at me.

I couldn't bring it up. I felt strange. You know, the nervous feeling you get when you want to ask a question but you're scared of the response or how you might look asking such a question. *Gosh, it's so much easier to just keep quiet,* I thought.

Later that evening we were watching a movie together and I thought I'll raise it after.

'Just a question…be honest with me. I know many men do.. do you watch pornography?' I asked hesitantly.

'No, I don't,' he said. He looked at me right in my eyes, his voice soft and genuine. 'I don't want porn darling. Why would I watch that when I have you?'

I was upset. Why was he denying it? I knew he was watching it.

The conversation continued as I told him to be honest with me.

'No Jasmine, I don't, but when you catch me watching it, that is when we can talk,' he responded. I didn't understand this response. It left me confused. I didn't know what to say next. When I catch him watching it? Should I tell him I actually saw it in his history? No, that would lead to another argument. I didn't get it, but at the same time I did. He was indirectly telling me he does watch it, but it would be a surprise if I ever caught him. I stayed silent, what more was there to say, I'd got the answer…

I was shocked by the situation. I felt betrayed. I wondered if I had imagined it all. It seemed out of character – a Christian man, who teaches the children at Sunday school. A scholarly man, who was well respected in church. It just didn't make sense.

I was deeply, deeply upset by this. Discovering this hidden side of his character seemed more than I could bear. I wondered whether I was overreacting.

I felt disgusted and ashamed. It was not just about him watching it, it was everything that came along with it. The secrecy surrounding it, his switching it off when I came into the room, waiting until he thought I was asleep and then picking up his phone. All I could think about was him wanting to watch it and me being in the way. I wanted honesty between us, trust, and communication. I wanted him to talk to me.

'Please, feel free to talk to me about anything. I want you to be open with me,' I said. I had noticed throughout the short period of time we had been married he rarely said anything about what was going on in his personal life. You know sometimes you feel tired, or exhausted about something going on, or happy and excited about your future. There was never anything he raised.

'Nothing is going on, but I will,' he'd respond.

I know men often struggle to talk about things, but I wanted a relationship where we could bring everything and anything to the table. Nick portrayed himself to be a sensitive husband who wanted to make his marriage work, and he would engage in conversations about the marriage, nodding and smiling whilst making suggestions. If I, however, told him he had hurt me or offered constructive feedback, he would tell me how hurt he was. Through word twisting, the issue I had brought up somehow became my fault at the end of the conversation.

Later, I would suffer the consequence of the silent treatment, another form of subtle retaliation. If I withdrew to protect myself, he explained that I was causing problems by being distant and rejecting him.

On one occasion, he opened up to me. 'Yes, I have watched porn,' he said.

'During the marriage?' I responded.

'Yes, during the marriage,' he said, looking down at his hands. I couldn't believe he'd admitted it to me. He looked sorry.

I stayed calm, of course. I wanted to know the exact reason why, and I had to stay calm and empathetic to get the answer. Was it truly because I wasn't satisfying my husband? 'Why do you watch it?' I asked.

'I don't know.' He looked to the left and to the right. I wanted to know the extent of this – was he addicted, or was he enjoying it?

Trying to say it in my calmest, most encouraging voice, I asked, 'Would you say it was an addiction?' I gave him time, and I stayed silent. I think I held my breath for a second as he thought about it. I finally saw a side to him I had never seen before. He was finally opening up to me.

'I guess it's boredom,' he said. 'I watch it during football halftime.' After hearing that, I didn't know what to think. *Where do you go from there?*

I decided to explain how it made me feel. I explained how I felt when I walked into the room, the feeling of unease as he quickly switched off his phone. Nothing was ever said. Maybe he thought I didn't know, but I knew.

The fact that he was hiding it was worse than him actually watching it. I asked if he could stop watching it, and he agreed. We hugged, and I believed I had finally connected with him. However, the porn continued, and when I later asked him again about it, he said he had never watched it while we were married. I could always tell when Nick had been watching it. He'd behave as someone who had something to hide but would become offended that I didn't trust him.

'You already admitted that you've watched it before, remember?' I said in absolute shock that we were back there. He sat still, probably trying to remember when and what he had told me.

'I don't watch it, not since we've been married,' he said.

'Don't you remember? You said you watch it during football halftime,' I responded, now out of annoyance. He was denying the facts of the situation and rewriting history, making me believe my memory was unreliable. In fact, I really tried hard to see if he could be right, but I knew we'd had that conversation. I knew I was not crazy. I knew it because when we'd had that conversation, I was happy. I remembered thanking God for a good conversation. I remembered the hug. I remembered the peace and honesty between us. I remembered every single detail.

'What are you talking about? I never said that. You're making things up,' he responded.

It was exhaustingly confusing. He always gave different answers to the same questions. Likewise, he would give different reasons for the same behaviours. Sometimes, he would admit it and say sorry; sometimes he would blame me; other times he'd deny it completely.

'Nick, you have forgotten you have told me…' I said.

It went silent, as he was thinking.

'Oh, I have watched it during our marriage,' he said. When I stood my ground, the truth once again came out. It was never easy. It was a tight fight between me and my emotions, me and my strength, me and my perception, and me and my memory. In fact, it was a tight fight between my being sane and my being crazy.

I tried on several occasions to discuss our marital problems and how him watching pornography made me feel; however, I left feeling deeply confused every single time. I made promises to work harder on myself and overlook issues whilst being mad at myself for feeling defensive. I often wondered if I were crazy and this was all my fault.

It was a sunny afternoon. The sun was shining, the road was busy, and it was a day to be happy, but I left the house crying. Where could I go?

We had had a horrendous argument, in which he raised all my previous flaws and wrongdoings that had led to disagreements. I was again labelled as having anger issues. 'You need to sort this out! It is not good for you and me also! Your anger is affecting me!' The way he articulated my flaws left me hopeless and speechless with nothing else to do but to find an escape. A part of me felt sorry for myself and all the thousands of women that were in my situation. Pregnant and in an emotionally or physically abusive relationship. I couldn't believe that this was really my life; that this was what my life had come to. It was like a good dream which had been shattered into pieces.

Unable to bear it any longer, I called my friend Stacey who lived down the road, a five-minute drive away, a ten-minute walk. I had left the house in a house dress; it was a dress I would not have worn out because my bra was showing. I had to hold the dress together because I had no time to change. The dynamic of the house had forced me out. I decided I would drive to avoid being seen, so I got into my car, tears rolling down my face. I put the key into the ignition, paused, and took it out. I wasn't ready to drive yet. I needed to be calm. I couldn't stop crying. It hurt because I was carrying a baby, and I felt like I was at the end of my tether. I didn't know what to do or where to go. I was lost. I cried and cried, then pulled myself together. I put the key into the ignition, put my seatbelt on, and started driving, praying that God would see me through and get me to Stacey's house safely. She had already responded to say that she wasn't home, but I didn't know where else to go, so I drove to her house.

I parked outside and just sat there, thoughts going on in my head. What would she say? What would she think? Should I tell her that I wasn't happy? Should I tell her what was going on? It was repeatedly said in church that if there are problems in your home, don't speak to anyone about it, especially your friends. There were many examples of women who spoke out about their problems, and that was the end of their marriage. Their friends stole their husbands, and the wives were left all alone, sad and depressed. I wondered how I could keep it all in. It was killing me on the inside, in my mind. My brain couldn't function clearly. Pathways of thoughts went in every direction. I needed to tell someone.

Tears continually rolled down my face, but I had been there long enough, so I decided to go back home. I didn't want to go back; I felt like running away. On several occasions, I thought about it. I'd just go to a hotel and switch off my phone. It'd be like I'd disappeared, but Mum would be so worried, and so would Jacklyn. They would probably get the police out looking for me, there would be search posts on social media…everyone would be worried, that wouldn't be right. With nowhere else to go, I went back home.

'One of us needs to be the man in this marriage,' I said to him. His emotions were too much. I could not deal with it. He was like a wounded soldier. I was emotional, and he was emotional – what on earth was going on? 'Did I marry a woman?' I said.

'You need to understand my feelings,' he responded. It was a lot. It was too much. The heavy weight of my issues, the pregnancy, the nausea, the heartburn, his emotions, his dilemma, the pornography, the denial, the phone – it was too much. It was overwhelming to have someone frequently feel or act like a victim in my life at that stage, and I couldn't cope with it all. Each day, I thought I had reached my breaking point, but I carried on.

It was dinner time. I asked if he wanted dinner, and he said no, so I stopped asking him. I realised that he didn't eat when he was unhappy. I told him I would not beg him to eat. I was not that type of woman, I explained.

In Nigerian movies, I saw how the women pleaded with their husbands to eat food, to be happy. 'I am not the Nigerian wife who will kneel down and beg for you to eat.' I went and ate alone, feeding myself and the little baby in my womb; he stayed upstairs and didn't eat.

The next day, he raised the fact he hadn't eaten since the day before.

'So? I told you to eat.' I really didn't want to fall into that pattern, him playing the victim when he was not the victim. Again, it was too much. Whenever he wasn't around, and I had an opportunity to cry, I cried. I hated everything.

'You know what they say about nagging wives,' he said.

This offended me. 'I do not nag,' I said. After pleading and begging with him to read the Bible and pray for me at the beginning of the marriage, I'd stopped, and I never asked him to do Bible study with me again. I stopped asking for a lot of things, especially when I was pregnant.

It was gaslighting. He was winding me up, making me feel as if I was the one in the wrong, and I couldn't take it. When I had told him to do the online course, it wasn't me nagging; rather, it was me trying to help lift him up and make him successful. I wanted to build him up, but he made me believe that all I was doing was nag. The truth is that I only wanted him to be a successful man.

He knew I was right – I don't nag. He never said it again.

I didn't realise his reactions were narcissistic. In fact, at that point, I didn't even know the meaning of the word, but it all made sense later, during the healing process when I began to realise what had truly happened. This kind of abuse is called covert – it's hidden and secret, and unfortunately, the manifestation of covert emotional abuse is difficult to spot, extremely hard to define, and therefore, impossible to confront.

He felt attacked when I contradicted him, questioned him, or told him he had done something wrong. I guess this was because it did not align with his inflated sense of self, his sense of entitlement, his denial, his delusions of grandeur, his grandiosity, his need for control, his narcissistic rage, and his low-level empathy; these are all reasons why he acted why he did. I knew something wasn't right when I cried in the shower and in the park, but I hadn't truly known, especially because I believed he was the man with whom I would spend eternity.

It made it extremely hard when no one saw what was going on. No one saw what was truly happening. Covert abuse covers all types of brutality, manipulation, and harm inflicted on another person, whether that harm leaves physical scars or not. The abuse, which is so difficult to identify by nature, requires people with a high emotional IQ to spot and respond to the abuse. At times, it's true that it's extremely hard to see this type of abuse, even with the help of counsellors and pastors.

Chapter 9

A Painful Experience

May 1st 2020, was the first time I wrote in my journal. I decided that I needed a gratitude journal, to write down one thing each day for which I was grateful. It wasn't just my gratitude journal, it was a mental health, stress management and wellbeing tool. It would keep me sane.

It was less than two months after I had said my vows in church. I was trying to find a technique to find peace, to make myself happy, to avoid being depressed or sad. It was hard, finding the one thing for which I was grateful every day. On some days, I wrote, 'Thank God for the gift of life.' I wrote that on days where there was nothing else to say. It was a horrible time. He would sit on his phone all day whilst I pleaded for the both of us to spend time together, to go for a walk together, just to have some fun.

He refused to go on walks. He said it was too cold, he was not born in this country, and he didn't like the cold, so I would go alone, walking around the commons behind my house, praying, taking in nature, and getting some peace. I always wondered what he was up to, why he couldn't just follow me.

'I'm going for a walk,' I said to him on one occasion.

Silence.

He was busy watching something on his phone.

I put on my jacket and left the room, left the house. I was so sad. I waited until I got to the commons and off the main road before I cried. The commons felt empty. There were just a few people. No one saw me. Tears fell down my face as I walked, lonely and sad – how did I allow this to become my life? I was upset, thinking that this was God's will for my life. I cried so much; my eyes were red, sore, and burning.

He called me.

I answered.

He asked where I was and apologised for not acknowledging me. He said he was coming to join me.

I was happy but still sad. I had cried for the last 20 minutes, wiping my tears away every time I saw someone, either a dog walker or two elderly people. I stood around, waiting for him to meet me.

He came. He didn't notice that I had been crying. He never really noticed anything. I had wiped all of my tears away, but if he had looked properly, maybe he would have noticed the watery eyes and the sadness on my face. Anyway, I was somewhat happy, and we continued the walk together. I thanked God that he had come out. *Thank you, Jesus*, I thought.

***

It wasn't always bad. He would clean and tidy the house and do things for me. Oh, he was a do-er – doing everything perfectly – and I appreciated him for that.

On one occasion, I asked him to go to the shop for me that would take around 45 minutes to an hour to get to. I explained that I was craving a snack, and they only sold it in that shop. I wanted to see whether he would go all that way to get me a snack at 10:30 p.m. at night.

He picked himself up, put on his coat, and asked me to check what time the shop closed so he could make sure he would make it in time. Whilst looking down at my phone, I thought, *Wow! He's really going to go.*

I told him it closed at 11 p.m.

He said he was going quickly, and he left the room.

'Nick, come back,' I said.

He walked back into the room.

'I was just joking,' I said. That was when I knew he would do anything for me.

He would wash up, hoover the whole house, take out the bins, and hang the clothes. He helped me out so much around the house. It was perfect, and I was grateful, but the emotional support was not there.

I appreciated the doing, but the lack of empathy was eating me up and destroying my mind, the very part of the body that kept me sane. I needed friendship and support; I needed love.

'He acknowledged me and spent time with me today,' I wrote in my journal on one occasion. Looking back now, all I really wanted was companionship, love between us, happiness, and a safe place, but there was no safe place with him. I didn't trust him. I blamed myself – did I have trust issues? Jasmine, just trust him.

I tried my best. I was in torment, wondering why I couldn't trust him. He was 'loving, kind, and had my best interests at heart,' according to him. Unfortunately, my weaknesses and insecurities grew larger and larger over the course of the marriage. I couldn't stand the thoughts in my mind.

I sought help. I messaged Pastor Daniel and told him I needed help, that I didn't trust Nick, and I wanted to know how I could trust him more.

He didn't respond. He later spoke with Nick and told him what I'd said. Nick was not happy and later that evening, he made sure I knew: 'How do you think it makes me look if you say you don't trust me?' he said.

'Yes, I don't, but I want to.' I wasn't sure why he was upset with me. Surely, he should hold me closer and say he wanted me to trust him more. Surely that was how it should be?

No, he was upset that I had admitted the truth to someone and had maybe hurt his ego and ruined his reputation.

'What have I done for you to not trust me?' He was upset and reversing the conversation onto me, leaving me to think it had been me, questioning myself.

We didn't speak that evening. He was upset, and so was I. It was hard not speaking to him or to anyone, and I felt lost and lonely. I was pregnant, dealing with my pregnancy emotions, and then I was also dealing with him.

***

December 24th, 2020 was the first Christmas Eve I spent in tears. I was 32 weeks pregnant. After exchanging words, I went downstairs to the living room whilst he stayed, lying down in the bed. The emotional abuse, however, was rampant. I cried throwing my pregnant self on the floor. I cried my eyes out. I'm sure he heard me, but he didn't come down.

Later that evening, he came down to see me. I had tears all down my face, my eyes were red, my heart was hurting, and I was feeling pain in my stomach. When he walked into the room, he didn't say anything but just looked at me.

'Go away!' I said as I cried. I didn't want to see him; I didn't want him near me. He turned around, opened the door and walked back upstairs without saying a word. As a woman, you want someone to hold you and say it's going to be okay. Although I didn't want him near, I thought it would have been nice if he had tried but he allowed me to cry whilst he walked back to bed.

He later told me he'd gone back upstairs because I had told him to.

I cried out to God to keep me and keep my baby safe. I was seriously worried about my health. No one could see I was suffering emotionally. I prayed that God would help strengthen my son and I. I cried and tried to make myself comfortable on the sofa so I could sleep.

The next morning, my eyes were so puffy, red, and stinging. Christmas breakfast was awkward. I looked like I had been to war and back.

He sat next to me. 'Please, just be happy,' he said, *but it just doesn't work like that*, I thought. I can't suddenly be happy. I can't suddenly forget how he treated me the night before. I had hardly slept. I'd spent all night crying, and now I was being told just to be happy. He told me he was sorry, and he pleaded with me to be happy.

I tried my best to smile. Gosh, it was so horrible, trapped in my own emotions, not knowing how I felt, with my fake smiles and broken heart – and this was God's will for my life? It was horrible. God, why?

Christmas was not an enjoyable experience at all. I gave him all of his presents whilst he gave me mine, a pair of small hoop earrings. I tried to be happy, but it was so hard. I felt caged. No one could see what I was going through, living at home with my mum, stepdad, and brother – could they not see?

I spoke to my mum, crying out to her. Her response was to pray, and all would be okay, so I did. I prayed to God to take hold of the marriage.

Did I deserve this? Was it my part to suffer in this life? Did I have to experience how life can bring you down on my own? Was it because I had lived an okay life so far? I wondered about this so many times. Was that my fate, my story, my destiny? Was that my reward for waiting until marriage to have sex? Was it payback for good works? Truly, my mind operated 24/7 in full motion, bringing different questions, scenarios, and thoughts to my brain. I felt like I was in prison, a prison in my mind and life, a prison I hoped to one day get out of, to one day walk free and be free.

Chapter 10

The Best Marriage

Our church services were on Zoom every night. Although I was tired, nauseated, and unhappy, I made it an absolute priority to tune into church services every night. I put on my camera and sat down so I could really be a part of the virtual online service. It was an hour in which I could escape from my worries and pain and be happy, connect with God, and pray with other people. Although I really enjoyed it, I wanted him to join in with me, but he didn't want to, and that was fine.

One evening, he sat next to me and said he would be with me for the virtual service, and I was happy.

'I really enjoyed tonight…you sitting with me, us praying together,' I said.

'Me, too,' he replied.

'Please, let's do it more often,' I said.

'We will sit together for the live service every night. That's what I want,' he said. He seemed genuine, and indeed, more or less every night after that, he came to sit with me on the bed for the live service. I'd never been happier. Most women sat by themselves. There were hardly ever any men present for the live church services apart from three or four, and there were no couples – just two others – but no other couples sat together on camera, and I was happy that he was joining me.

Nick and I were seen as role models for Christian marriage. Our marriage appeared perfect. There was a service on marriages, and Nick and I were one of the couples on the panel. It was Nick and I with five other couples. We should not have been on the panel, and I knew it. We had been together for seven months at the time, and we were asked to speak about our marriage, how we got through our problems, how it had been, and how we had met. I wondered what it would be like if I'd have said the truth. I wondered what would happen if I opened my mouth and told our fellow online church members that I was unhappy and cried so much during the seven months we'd been together. What would they say? What would they think? What would Pastor Daniel say? Imagine if I cried on camera and the whole world saw me.

I held myself together and tried to be calm. That particular night we were not on good terms, we were not speaking for a reason I cannot remember, so when it came to 9 p.m., he came to sit next to me on the bed, and we put on a face for the church to see. As we sat there, talking about our marriage, I knew I was living a fake life. We were genuinely struggling – or should I say, I was struggling. We needed help.

A question came about how we handled disagreements, and I couldn't lie. 'We are still working on that, praying that God will help us,' I said. I saw a few people smiling and nodding their heads, as if they understood and were thankful for the honesty. For the hour we were live, I was nervous, my hands were sweating, my heart was beating out of my chest. *What would they ask us? Would people know that I was sad and unhappy?* I wondered.

We made it successfully through the first and second day and did not speak at all on the final day. It was awkward. He came to sit next to me for the live service, and we started. We were in the spotlight again. We maintained an image of having it all together during the service, but when it finished, we sat in silence with nothing to say. Why had we been chosen as the best couple, a couple to put on the panel? I don't know. Was it because we were always on the virtual services together? Or did Pastor Daniel find our marriage worthy? I don't know.

After each session, I went to my mum. 'How did I look? Did I look happy?' I asked. As I was pregnant and still badly nauseated, I don't think she thought twice when I asked her the question. I pushed through the nausea and went live every day, even on days I was severely sick.

There were more silent times; the silent treatment was horrible. On one occasion, we didn't speak for four days. It was my baby in my womb that gave me peace, that made me know all would be okay. The silent treatment, or stonewalling as it's known, is just another way to punish a person, making them feel unworthy and unseen. He would make it very clear that he was making a sacrifice to help me. He wouldn't speak to me, withholding comfort, love, and intimacy to punish me. It was heart-breaking, and in all honesty, if it was not for the little feet growing inside me, I could have given up at any moment.

Chapter 11

Help!

'If only he could just physically abuse me,' I said to my mum on the phone, 'then everyone would know what I was going through. People would be able to see it.' I knew he would never hit me. That was not his approach. That was not his tactic. My mum wasn't happy when I said that; she didn't understand. She also didn't understand the stress and depression. She didn't know what was happening or the true meaning behind my words. I didn't blame her. A lack of understanding is one of the reasons why women and their families or friends might not recognise abuse right away. It's only when it gets extremely serious, when the effects start to show and the mind starts to wither, that it's noticed there is an issue.

'Why would you say you want him to physically abuse you? Don't say that again.' She didn't understand. I don't believe I truly understood what was happening either. I just knew that whatever it was, it was not healthy, and it was extremely dangerous.

Nick would never hit me. I believed it would never get physical. That was not him. However, without ever hitting me, he rendered me powerless.

Emotional abuse can be subtle and deceptive or explicit and manipulative. Either way, it eats away at the victims' self-esteem, and they begin to doubt their perceptions and reality. That's exactly what happened. He said he really loved me, but when I cried, he sat and ignored me. Is this what marriage was like?

I felt trapped – what could I do? What could I say? I continued to pray – that was all I could do, right? I wondered if it would be this way forever. Surely, I had to do more than just pray, I thought. I tried my best to make things work, making time for us to spend together, to connect and go deeper. This led to us having some really good moments, but when it was bad, it was really bad.

After another argument, I left the house in the pouring rain. I put my umbrella up, not knowing where I was going yet. I held my stomach and felt the little man inside me kick. This gave me joy and peace to keep going. I walked to the bus stop, with tears rolling down my face. There was an elderly woman sitting down. She saw I was pregnant, and she asked if I wanted to sit down.

'No, I'm okay,' I said. Thank God for the facemasks, I thought, as she could not see I was crying.

I got onto the bus, found a seat on the lower deck, and closed my eyes, trying to keep the tears from pouring out. As I closed my eyes, I zoned out. My mind had stopped with the racing thoughts, the questions, and the doubts.

'Sorry Miss, this is the last stop,' I heard a man say. I must have been on the bus for over an hour. I hadn't realised.

'Oh, thank you,' I responded as I hurriedly got up and walked towards the door. I didn't know where I was going, but at least I wasn't home, I thought. I couldn't cope with the atmosphere, the silent treatment, the arguments, the phone. I couldn't deal with any of it, none of it at all. It was all too much for me to handle.

I walked with the rain pouring down, my feet soaked. I held my stomach a few times to feel little man kick – this was a frequent action; I needed to know he was okay. If he was okay, I was okay. They say happy mum, happy baby. I wasn't happy, but I tried to look after myself the best I could, to make myself smile, to make myself happy.

Walking into Greggs, I decided to buy something to eat because I hadn't eaten yet. Pregnancy cravings kicked in, and I bought two vegan sausage rolls and two vegan doughnuts, and I ate on the street. There were no seats available due to the lockdown.

As I walked, I was tired. People looked at me. Seeing my stomach, I imagined they thought, 'Bless her.'

I walked to WH Smith to look at books. What other way is there to use your time than to look at books, read the blurb, read the first page, and think about how interesting the book might be. I had been standing and walking for so long my legs were weak. There were no seats at all and nowhere to just sit down and rest but, the pain in my legs and back was better than experiencing what I'd experienced at home.

After spending some time at WH Smith, I had found four books in which I was interested, and I went to pay for them. After paying, I continued to walk. Where should I go next? The majority of the shops were closed, and if a shop was open, it had no seats. I was becoming extremely tired, and I needed to sit down.

I messaged two friends from church – they are sisters – to see if I could visit them.

They said they were free, so I went round. Unable to walk anymore, I got an Uber. When I reached their house, it was nice. I relaxed. I was happy. I was finally sitting down in a house that was not mine, where people were happy, and the atmosphere was calming.

They asked how I was doing. I thought it was obvious I was not doing okay, but it wasn't, so I just stuck with the happy routine.

We watched a movie, which was great. I really enjoyed their company. We had dinner, roasted potatoes, and spicy vegetables. It was delicious. I then realised a vibration in my pocket. My phone was ringing. It was him. At that point, I realised it was my first call all day.

I decided I was not going to answer. How awkward would it be if I answered and ended up crying because the conversation hadn't gone well? I avoided the embarrassment, thinking, 'Let me just continue being happy.' Of course, I wouldn't sleep there that night – I would eventually have to go back to face him. I would deal with it then. I was happy to see him calling me, though. Truthfully, I was happy. It showed that he did have a heart, and he did have some compassion for his pregnant wife. I was happy to see his call, yet I chose not to answer. In all honesty, I was scared he would tell me off that I'd been gone all day and not contacted him. *Maybe I'd caused him to feel anxious and worried*, I thought. Funny, right? Things were so easily switched over to being my fault that I could see how I could be blamed in any situation.

It got to be 7 p.m. I had been out the house since morning, and it was now time to head back home, but I didn't want to go. Please, please, Lord – I don't want to go. But I had to. It was my house, and I had nowhere else to go.

When I got back home, I stayed downstairs. My mum was doing a client's hair, so I stayed and talked with them. When it was finally time for me to go upstairs, I felt anxiety rush through my body, like a sudden outburst of rain. As I went upstairs, I thought about what he had been doing all day – one of my constant thoughts as he laid on the bed with his phone in his hand.

When I opened the bedroom door, he stood up. There were candles in the room, a bottle of non-alcoholic wine, and Christmas decorations had been put up. He apologised to me, told me he'd missed me so much as I had been gone all day. He said he couldn't eat as he wasn't sure whether I had eaten. As he continued talking, I looked around the room and smiled. I thought it was nice and really sweet of him to do this for me; apology accepted. I was tired and exhausted, and we'd moved on. Emotionally, I was on a cycle, in up and down emotional turmoil, ready to explode, but that time had not come yet.

THE UNSEEN VEIL

140

Chapter 12

Death and Life

It was Thursday evening on January 5th when my sister called me to give me the news that our dad had passed away. I had just finished work, exhausted from a long day and extremely tired. Nick was in another room. 'Dad's dead,' she said.

I could hear it had taken a lot of strength to say that, and she was holding herself together, but then her voice cracked, and the crying started.

Exhausted and mentally ill, I sat in silence, not knowing what to say or do. All I could think was that I would never see him again, and he will never see his grandson. I didn't know what to say, so I responded, 'I will call you back.' I was not sure how to take the news. I had not experienced death so closely before, so I didn't know how to react.

Unlike my sister, I didn't cry. It was strange. I was confused by my response.

Nick came into the room. I told him the news. He came and sat by me and hugged me. He looked at me. 'Why are you not crying?' he asked. I guess he thought it was strange; I did too.

He spoke about when he'd lost his dad, and I sat and listened. After some time, I just wanted peace. I didn't want to continue listening to his story. It wasn't helping and I didn't really know why it was necessary at that point in time. I decided to go and shower. The shower was my safe space, and I needed to digest what was going on.

I wasn't comfortable with Nick. He had made me cry so many times that it felt strange to have him comforting me now. I went into the bathroom, put some music on as usual, and stepped into the shower.

Holy Spirit, Fill This Place is the song I listened to. I sang along, held my stomach, and allowed the water to run down my head. I closed my eyes and was taken to another place. My thoughts were distant. I thought about Dad's last moments, how he was by himself, how I hadn't been there for him. I thought about all the memories we shared together, all of the Sunday dinners.

I sang and sang. When I was done, I knew I had to get out and go back to the room. *Great*, I thought.

I went back to the room, and he sat there in silence, looking at me, probably looking for any sign of tears. He stared at me. I sat down, and he hugged me. His attention was different. His attitude told me I should be crying. A few tears dripped down my face, and he told me it was okay.

He looked sad, too. He talked about all of the times he had spoken to my dad, and I sat and listened, but it went in one ear and out the other.

The death of my dad showed me there was an immense amount of beauty in life, that there was something to be grateful for, even in the bad. It changed my perception of life, who I was, and the preciousness of life all around me, including my little baby in my womb. There was light in the darkness. I held my stomach, grateful for the beginning of the new life inside of me.

I was due to give birth in a few weeks, so I started writing my birth plan for labour, I came across the birthing partner section – how I wished I could have had my mum with me during labour, but it was a lockdown, and the birthing policies had changed, so you could only have one person with you which meant one birthing partner. I explained to him that often, mothers-to-be in labour get angry or emotional with their spouses, that it was a common and not surprising situation that occurred in the labour ward. Women shouted and screamed at their partners because the pain was unbearable, and while I'm not sure why this happens, I knew it happened and could possibly happen when I was in labour. After I explained to him, I pleaded with him that he should not get upset with me if I am emotional and not to beat me down because this was normal. I added that if he got upset, Mum would be outside in the car, ready to come in. Of course, he was not happy with the fact that I'd planned for my mum to come in, but it was really me preparing myself for a situation that could, unfortunately, happen. I had already experienced this throughout my pregnancy. He was always getting upset with my emotions – what made giving birth any different? I was worried, and I needed to know I had a plan. I could have planned this without telling him; maybe I should have, but I wanted him to know. He didn't understand my emotions in pregnancy – how on earth would he understand it when I was giving birth? I thought he would probably tell me off.

He was upset, and we argued that night. Another evening of silence.

I wrote my birth plan alone in the room. He sat on the opposite end of the bed, on his phone. He didn't want to get involved, and at that point, I didn't mind. I was used to doing things alone.

Luckily, my labour experience was peaceful. I had given birth to a handsome bouncing baby boy, which we named Zian. There were no arguments. No drama. Thank God! Mum was on FaceTime the whole time; it was nice. Nick held the phone, speaking to Mum at times. He did well, although he kept asking why the nurses hadn't asked him if he wanted to eat.

'It's the mother who needs the food,' the midwife would say. I know he was joking around, but it wasn't funny because he said it more than once. *Just be the man*, I wanted to say. Appreciate the midwives for asking your wife what she wanted to eat and for bringing her food, and pull yourself together. I couldn't stand to hear him make that joke again, but it continued – when discussing the labour, he would say that he didn't have any food.

144

One week after Zian was born, was the day of my dad's funeral. 24th February 2021. I was given the eulogy to read a few weeks before. I had only practised it that morning as I hadn't had time previously. We were sat towards the back of the church, Zian, Nick and my mum. It was now time for me to read the eulogy. I stood up gently as I was still in pain from childbirth. I had torn and had stitches which were excruciatingly painful. I walked slowly towards the front of the church. I stood at the alter and picked up the microphone. I wanted to say the first word, but I struggled. It was hard; the words just wouldn't come out, and I started to cry.

I couldn't believe what was going on. I stood still, and it was silent as everyone looked at me.

The relationship with my dad had been complicated as he'd suffered from mental health issues; however, he had the biggest heart. I loved him, and I knew he loved me. Now he was gone.

That evening, Nick was on the phone with someone as I walked into the room with Zian.

'They just walked into the room,' he said, and that was it – he was off the phone.

'Oh, I thought you were on the phone – why did you get off?'

'The conversation ended,' he said. It was strange and weird. Why had the conversation ended so abruptly after I'd walked into the room with our son? I didn't understand.

'Should we leave so you can get back on the phone?' I asked.

'No, it's finished,' he said, scrolling down his Facebook page.

He told me he was speaking to his brother. I didn't believe him.

My emotions were already on a high that day, I had been feeling emotionally worn-out and drained. I didn't feel safe, not with him, not in that room, not in the house, not at all.

The emotional toll had made me feel moody, irritable and on edge.

'Why are you acting like this? I told you I was talking to my brother,' he said angrily. He was not happy because I was not happy. I didn't believe he was talking to his brother because I didn't understand why the conversation had suddenly ended. The argument continued until I broke down and cried.

I realised that he didn't even consider it had been my dad's funeral a few hours ago, and I was extremely emotional. It was one week postpartum, and I was still bleeding heavily and weak. I was stressed and just needed someone to hold me tightly, someone who would make me feel better and take away my worries and pain.

'You are so inconsiderate. Today was my dad's funeral, and you are arguing with me,' I said. I couldn't understand him, his thinking, or his thought processes. He was playing the victim when he was not the victim.

Again, that evening, we hardly spoke. I tuned into the virtual church service and put on my camera to hold myself together. If I were live, I wouldn't start crying. I would put on a face and be happy. I also held my son, trying too hard, when, all of a sudden, I realised that I couldn't be bothered. I was tired, and I needed a break…from everything.

I switched off the camera, and we listened to the live service, not saying a word to each other. He sat with me, but it was awkward. I distracted myself with our son, changing his nappy and breastfeeding him. He became my safe space. Doing things with him distracted me from the isolation I felt in my marriage.

'Thank God for you, Baby Zian,' I said.

Because he had low empathy, it was difficult for him to understand where I was coming from. Whenever I expressed how I was feeling, it hurt by his behaviour. He didn't want to see it my way. He never understood why his behaviour or actions had hurt me. As far as he was concerned, I was complaining and treating him unfairly.

It felt as if I was being framed. The constant gaslighting made me second guess my version of reality. He labelled my self-defence reactions as vile aggression against him. *How dare you react or challenge me? You deserve to cry. You deserve to be unhappy. When you've cried enough, I will apologise; until then, cry*, I can imagine him thinking. Of course, me being emotional, pregnant, and stressed, I would cry. He would often say, 'You're so sensitive and unfair!'

Whilst I don't want to label Nick, in my healing and recovery process, I read up on narcissism and emotional abuse and as I read, I realised how much of his behaviour was synonymous with what I was reading. I began to understand that people with these traits cannot accept that they are not perfect. They are also incredibly fragile when facing the idea that perhaps they have done something wrong, especially if others can see it.

Therefore, if there's a conflict, they will do anything and everything to maintain the fantasy that they are always good, all the while perceiving the other party as evil. This is what always happened: I was the wrong one. Always.

It reminds me of when we would argue after Zian was born. He wouldn't speak to me but just go straight downstairs with the sterilising kit and start washing all the bottles. I thought, *What good is it if we don't have that friendship, a relationship, joy, and happiness?* After researching about emotional abuse, it all made sense.

Chapter 13

Tearful Celebrations

It was April 11th, 2021. My birthday. I sat in the car. Zian was home with Grandma. I had cried so much I fell asleep and woke up to the sound of beeping. My sister, brother-in-law, Michael, nieces, and nephew had just driven past me. They stopped when they noticed I was in the car and beeped at me.

When I woke up, I saw them and smiled. I was always happy to see them. Michael lowered his window, I lowered mine, and I explained to them that I didn't know I had fallen asleep.

They dropped the children off at my house, and my sister came back with two mugs of tea in each hand, one for me and one for herself.

As I sipped on the tea, I explained to her why I was sat fast asleep in a parked car at the side of the road, on my 26th birthday.

Yet another occasion had been ruined. It could have been me that had ruined it, but at the same time, I knew – I definitely knew – I hadn't got over all the trauma, the tears, and arguments from the year. Everything was going too fast. There was no time to slow down, no time to actually take a moment and pause, have a break. There was no time to stop the merry-go-round of emotional torture, irritation, annoyance, and self-doubt.

I had done a photoshoot for my birthday the day before. I went out in the morning to get my makeup and hair done, knocking on the door when I got home, all glammed up for the photoshoot. He came to open the door. He didn't even look at me. He just opened the door and walked back upstairs.

My heart. I'd had my makeup done – *no time for tears, honey*, I thought to myself. You need to go and get dressed up.

I ignored him. I didn't want to ruin yet another occasion. I just wanted to make myself happy.

My decorator was downstairs, setting up and getting everything ready for the shoot. I joined her and made sure I had a good time. She asked if Nick would be joining us for the photos, and I said, 'Maybe later. Let's just continue for now.'

Forty minutes passed. I went upstairs for an outfit change, and that's when he noticed me and told me I looked beautiful. I went back downstairs for the shoot and continued taking pictures. He stayed upstairs, probably on his phone.

Chapter 14

Let's Try a New Approach

'If you treat me this badly in my family home, let's stay with your family. Let's stay with your brother. Maybe you will treat me better there,' I said to him. His brother had a spare room in their house, and I figured it would be better to go there. Since I couldn't speak to anyone in his family about what was going on, I decided it would be better for us if we were in their presence.

Nick apologised for everything, explaining that he had now figured it all out. He said it was pride and ego that had got the better of him. He explained how sorry he was and that he would make things work if we could just stay where we were, at my mother's house.

In the back of my mind, I wondered why he didn't want to go so badly. The more he went on about treating me better at my mother's house, the more I was determined to go to his brother's.

'You can treat me better there,' I would say. 'Let's have a change of scenery, something different,' I explained to him. There's a saying in African culture that when you marry, you go to your husband's house. I explained to him that I should be in my husband's house anyway, and therefore, we should be staying with his family rather than mine.

His sister-in-law messaged me and sent me a picture of the room: no bed, just a mattress on the floor. I thought it was fine. I had everything in front of me at my mother's house, and it had been horrible. *It would be better to not have a bed and to be treated well*, I thought. In all honesty, I would not have minded sleeping on the floor.

We packed all our stuff. I asked him to pack all his things, literally every single item. 'Pack it all,' I said. I was fed up with being treated badly and knew the marriage could not continue in my mother's house. I had cried too many times, and it was affecting my mum. I could see she was not happy about seeing her daughter cry all the time.

We packed our bags and left for his brother's house. I was sad it had come to that, but I was happy and felt brave for doing it. I was sacrificing everything for peace, happiness, a good marriage, and to be treated well.

When we arrived, it was nice. His brother has three young children, and they ran up to me, excited to see their cousin, our boy Zian. We put all the things in our one bedroom and settled in.

We had a nice chat that evening, and I realised there was a difference. He left his phone out of sight and didn't touch it once. I couldn't believe it. He asked me if I was okay and wanted to eat. He made sure I was comfortable. He made sure I was happy. It was such a lovely time, and it brought a smile to my face. Things were going to finally change.

The second day we were there, I handed my son to his sister-in-law. I had just finished breastfeeding him, and he was falling asleep. I gave him to her and thought she was just going to hold him; however, she didn't. What she did next surprised me: she stretched his arms, pulling his arms back and stretched his legs, pulling his legs down.

'Oh, aunty, please, stop,' I said. I didn't like it. It's Nigerian tradition to stretch a baby when he is being bathed, but he was not in the bath, and I was not okay with it.

She continued. One second later, Zian was hanging upside down, head to the ground and legs in the air. I was devastated and shocked. It all happened so quick; I didn't know what to do. She then handed Zian back to me and said she will do it properly when she baths him. From that moment onwards, I knew I couldn't stay there, but what about the marriage? Did I go back to being abused? What should I do? I was so confused. I spoke to Nick and explained that I wasn't happy with what his sister-in-law had done. He explained that he thought we should go back to my mum's house. I was not surprised.

I insisted that I did not want to go back because of how he treated me there. He then suggested that we should get our own place, a one-bedroom apartment or studio room. I feared what it would be like if it was just us alone. At that moment, I realised I was fighting a losing battle. I had moved there because of the lion, and now there was a tiger, so I'd have to move back.

For my son's sake, we moved back to my mum's house. This could not – it just could not – continue. I was hurt. I had not yet healed, emotionally and physically from childbirth. This never-ending rollercoaster of high ups and extremely low downs was exhausting. The rollercoaster consisted of periods of closeness and periods of distance. The period of closeness drew me in – he was kind, loving, and once again, the man to whom I had said 'yes' to marriage. Then things would change, and he was distant, silent, and negative. My mind was everywhere; I had no peace.

'I will tell your family. I will tell them how you treat me, how you make me feel, how you've been treating me during this pregnancy,' I said to him.

'No, don't tell them. Don't. I'm just trying to protect you. If you speak to them, they won't see you the same way again. They will look at you differently.' Somehow, I believed him. I believed he was protecting me from his family, but why would they view me differently? I wondered. It was as if I was a girl from nowhere who he had built and lifted up on a pedestal to his family, and now I feared they would no longer see me that way.

'Nick why would they see me differently?' I needed an answer. I needed clarity. I didn't understand.

'I know what's best for you, and it is not a good idea,' he responded. That was the end of the conversation.

He made me believe that everything he did and said was for me when, in reality, he didn't want me to speak up about what was happening, what his pregnant wife was going through. He made me believe that he loved me so much. He made me and everyone else believe he was the best husband, so if I doubted him, I would look crazy, like what I was experiencing was not real. How on earth could I be right and everyone else be wrong?

I didn't speak out. In the back of my mind, I thought I would just pack a bag and go to his sister's house, sit there, and cry. Thank God I didn't, given what I know now about old school African mentality. They might not have seen anything wrong with Nick, but they might have blamed my pregnancy: 'You know, the hormones are making you like this,' I imagined them saying, but I was fed up with my mum always seeing me upset. I know seeing me cry broke her. I wanted his family to see, to know exactly what was going on. Maybe they would talk to him. Maybe they would tell him to look after me. Maybe they would discipline him.

'You know you can talk to us about anything,' his sisters had said to me on one occasion. Nick had been on the phone with his sisters, and they asked to speak to me.

'Thank you, aunty,' I responded – his sisters were much older than me, so I referred to them as aunty rather than sisters or by name. I wondered whether they knew I was sad and depressed. I wondered what had made them say that. Could I really speak to them? What would Nick say? I wondered what was going on in his mind when they'd said that. Did he wonder why they would say that? So many thoughts, no one to share them with.

'Okay, aunties, thank you.' That was it, just like that. A moment of hope had gone by, and they never said anything like that again and neither did I.

On one occasion, I called them. The argument had been too much, and I was ready for them to intervene and help. They were women. They would understand. One of them had two children – surely they would tell their brother to look after me properly and treat me well.

When I called them, all I could say was to ask them to please come over. Please come to the house. One of his sisters wanted to speak to Nick, so I gave him the phone, but he said nothing. Silence – he did not want to talk.

Right away, he called Pastor Daniel and asked if he could come round.

I explained the situation to him and explained that I had called Nick's sisters, and they were currently on their way.

He told me that was the wrong move, and I should call them to tell them not to come and tell them all was okay.

Why, I thought? Why can't they know? Why can't they help? Anyway, I called them. 'Sorry, aunty, don't come. All is sorted.' I cried. It was horrible, I was being silenced, I didn't know who to turn to. My mum was there, but she was not there. She didn't know the torture and pain in my mind.

My mum was trying her best to make sure things worked, encouraging me that she knew best with scriptures and prayers. I don't blame her – she wanted to see it work.

'I wish I could just drink something and kill myself,' I said to my mum. There was no escape, knowing that this would continue and go on forever. My marriage was killing me. It was torture. What else could

I do? I had to endure it, but it was hard. When enduring the pain of fire, it becomes too much after a while, and the fire begins to burn, becoming extremely hot.

Mum was shocked at my comment. She didn't understand.

Nick and I argued at night, and I didn't know what to do. I went to the bathroom and called a deaconess from church. I told her we had been arguing. She comforted me and told me to take it easy, that I should be resting my post-partum body. It was late, after 12 a.m. or so.

After the phone call with her, I looked for a number to dial. I knew there were numbers one could call to seek help. A helpline, a number for depression, sadness, emotional trauma, and suicidal thoughts. I found a number and called the line. It rang, finally, 'hope', I thought. Finally, someone who would understand what was going on, but what would I say? *Would* they understand? I wanted to speak to someone, a professional, someone who didn't know us about what was happening, someone who wouldn't tell me I was being over-sensitive or emotional.

The phone kept ringing, but I felt as if I was not worthy, and the call was not justified. He hadn't hit me, so the abuse was not 'bad enough'.

I cut the connection.

Chapter 15

Buried Alive

Since then, the atmosphere between us was cold. On one particular morning, the argument started.

'You are just unhappy in life. It's not me; it's you,' he said.

Here we go again, I thought.

One month after our baby was born, I was bleeding heavily and still feeling weak. I thought the bleeding was normal at the time, but it was only much later that I had realised that it was more serious than I had thought, I don't know what had caused it, but I reckoned it was stress. I hadn't stopped bleeding since I had given birth.

'I don't want to live in this house, but we aren't going back to your brother – can we please just have a break? Can you go and stay with your sister so I can have some time to think?' I asked him. Unfortunately, I no longer felt safe with him being at my mum's house because that was where the emotional abuse had happened. It was no longer a safe space. I had cried too many times on the bathroom floor. I had memories of sleeping in the spare room, emotionally drained. Whenever I walked the corridor, I feared going into our bedroom. It was becoming too much. I needed a change or a change needed to happen.

He said, 'I'm not going without Zian,' I couldn't believe he'd said that. Zian needed me. He needed his mum. We argued and argued until we couldn't argue any more.

Zian was sleeping, and I used the time to get into the shower. My safe place.

He left for work, and there was no goodbye. No hugs. No kisses.

As per usual, I cried in the shower. I cried, creaming my body. I cried all day. I tried to maintain my peace so I could put myself together and look after our baby. Whilst he was at work, he sent me a message about a flat for rent and told me to call the number to enquire, but I didn't respond. We'd had a heated argument in the morning, and I thought I would rather wait for him to get home so we could speak.

When he got home, he asked why I hadn't responded.

I explained that I hadn't responded because we'd had an argument, and I wanted us to resolve it.

He took off his jacket, looked at me eye to eye, and said, 'What argument? What are you talking about?' It was at that very point I knew he was trying to make me lose my mind.

I put my hands on my head, shocked and disgusted about what was happening. 'Nick, I am not losing my mind. We argued this morning.' I'd cried all day. *We had definitely argued*, I told myself as my mind raced as to what, exactly, was happening. I wasn't going to be manipulated or made to look crazy.

'We argued!' I exclaimed.

He looked at me as though I was losing my mind.

Was I losing my mind? Had I brought this upon myself? There was a side of me that kept me strong that knew I was sane. That side was stronger than the other side, the side that believed the lies and thought I was, indeed, crazy.

It was at that moment he went downstairs to tell my mum that I needed help and he just wanted to help me.

My heart pounded and raced. What was going on? After the exchange of argument, I told him to leave, and again, he wouldn't go. I had finally got to that place of surrender. I had finally let go of all attempts to change his character and repair the relationship. It was hard to see that he wasn't abusing me because he wanted to help me, but rather because he felt entitled to treat me that way. He did not see anything wrong with the way he treated me, so what could I do? If I stayed in the marriage, what on earth would happen to me? Would I sit on the sofa, crying every night? Would I find myself in a mental health unit? I had no idea.

It was not only emotional abuse, but it was also psychological abuse, I needed to run and run as fast as I could. I was ready to start a new chapter of my life, one of liberty, serenity, and joy.

The argument continued, and when he called me a hypocrite, I knew I couldn't do it anymore. What could I do to get him out? What could I do for this to just be over with? An idea came to my mind: why not call the police?

'If you won't go, I will call the police,' I said.

He stayed silent and seated.

He looked at me in the eye and didn't say a word.

I dialled 999 whilst my mum shouted, 'Jasmine, don't call the police!'

Nick sat there like a child, completely still, looking at me to see what I might do. I knew I needed to call the police. If I didn't, it would go on forever – how would I ever be free?

I looked at Mum as she fought for her son-in-law. I thought that if I didn't call the police, I would always be trapped in the marriage, that never-ending, emotional rollercoaster, an ongoing, emotional train journey, never knowing which stop to get off at – would it be a good stop or a bad stop? I'd had no downtime to heal emotionally, and I was fed up.

People could not see what was going on, and I was trapped in a prison of silence with broken things all around me. I felt like a prisoner in my own home. I felt like a dog on a chain, and I couldn't get it off. I needed to be set free and released to heal, rebuild, and recover.

After calling the police, he left immediately. The relief! I was finally at peace. Wow, he had gone, I thought to myself. Finally.

The peace didn't last long; he was back in my house. When he had left, he called Pastor Daniel who told him to go back home. Back to me. Pastor Daniel explained to Nick that he saw a vision of me committing suicide. So he was back in the house. My mum had let him in.

He came upstairs to the bedroom and told me the reason he'd come back.

'Pastor Daniel had a vision you had committed suicide…and that is why I am here,' he said.

'Okay,' I responded, wondering if there was anything more he wanted to say.

He said nothing.

I was scared by the vision, not because of what Pastor Daniel had seen, but because I could see how possible it was. I explained to Nick how I felt. I explained that the feelings were true. The more he didn't say anything, the more I got upset and angry. The whole time I spoke, he looked away and didn't face me. My mum had heard me practically crying my eyes out. She came in the room and asked what was going on. And just like he always did before, he said, 'I don't know Ma. She just keeps going on.'

I was shocked.

'Nick, do you want me dead?' I asked. There was no response. I know it's a deep question, but him staying silent was even deeper.

'Do you want me dead?' I asked him five times.

He didn't respond. He didn't even look at me. His eyes were fixated on my mum. Honestly, it was a scary and crazy moment. It was like he was captivated by an unknown force. Here physically but not spiritually.

'Well, I will never do it,' I said, as I responded to my own questions. I have a beautiful son who needs his mum, and I have a beautiful life ahead of me. So, I'm not going to kill myself. He shrugged and didn't say a word. I couldn't stand the lack of empathy. I really needed him out of the house. I told him he needed to go. My mum and stepdad came to speak to him. My stepdad offered to drop him home as it was late. He declined and said he would take public transport. He left that night at 1 a.m.

It was only later I realised he had been upset and angry that I had called the police and that's why he acted that way. I guess it must have been the pride. I can imagine him saying, '*My wife*, called the police on *me*.'

The next couple of days were a blur as I tried to process what had happened.

A few days later, I received a call from Pastor Daniel. I was happy as it had been quiet, and I didn't know what to think. When I picked up the phone, he explained that he had spoken to Nick and his sisters and now he was reaching out to me to hear my side of the story. I didn't know where to start. Where could I possibly start?

'I don't know what exactly to say, but I felt emotionally drained.' That was the best way to start. I continued, 'It's been horrible, and honestly, I wondered how I would be able to continue.' I went on about the arguments, the pregnancy, and the year I'd had. I poured out my heart about how I was feeling, how I used to cry, day and night, and how I often felt, and I started crying on the phone. I couldn't hold it back. The damage was still raw. The blood was still fresh. I cried on the phone as I continued to explain what had happened and how I felt. It was after that call I decided to take the advice I later saw on a support group on Facebook: be very careful who you pour your emotions out to; counsellors are good, but some may leave you feeling crazier than before you start.

Pastor Daniel started speaking: 'I regret joining you together.'

When I heard those words, I was shocked, heartbroken, and shattered. This was the pastor that had said Nick was God's will for my life. This was the pastor in whom I had total trust and faith, who had – on numerous occasions – told me Nick would look after me and not harm me. He was the pastor who had told me he prayed to God and saw Nick as my husband.

As I only wanted to do God's will, I couldn't believe my ears. I was, once again, back on the never-ending rollercoaster, and I didn't know what was going on. My heart started to beat faster and my hands started to shake. I became anxious about how the rest of the conversation would go. He went on to explain that he is only having this conversation with me so that when people ask him what he did as a pastor, he can say he did something. The more the conversation went on, the deeper I went into a deep hole. I felt vulnerable once again and at this point, I didn't know what my next move would be.

'What I would say to you, Jasmine, is that you need to see a counsellor, not me, a practitioner.'

'Okay, Pastor,' I said, my voice shaking.

I was completely speechless.

I mentioned the pornography to him. His response surprised me. He said he had asked Nick about it. I'm not sure when he knew and when he had asked Nick. I guess things get around somehow. Pastor Daniel responded with, 'No, Nick told me he does not watch it.'

'I asked him three times if he watches pornography. I told him that he should answer correctly and, if not, the wrath of God will strike him,' he said.

Deep I know.

'He said 'no' all three times, so Jasmine he does not watch pornography,' he continued.

I couldn't believe what I was hearing. I was lost for words at this point. Later, I wished I had spoken up and told him about the time Nick had been honest with me and actually admitted it or when I had seen it on his phone, but I didn't think about it at the time and stayed silent. This issue on pornography in marriages and in the church will have to be a completely separate book! It's something that needs to be addressed and not kept under the carpet.

Pastor Daniel always called me his baby girl. He said he loved me. He had two children: a daughter, and a son. He told me he loved me like he loved his children. He said it again in the conversation.

'You know you are my baby girl,' he said.

'Yes, and you would never like your daughter to go through this,' I responded with breaks in my voice.

'No, she will never ever go through this, never, there are things in place, she will never go through this,' he said.

The words were bitter and sour. They stung. I wondered what he meant when he said she would never go through this. I wondered whether he had truly understood what I had gone through and didn't want his daughter to experience the same or if he just meant a divorce. Either way the conversation was toxic and deteriorating for my mental health.

He thanked me for all the help I had done for the church and wished me all the best…it was like a goodbye.

I was confused.

I didn't blame him. He didn't understand. Sometimes, people don't, and that is fine now, but at the time, it wasn't so good. I needed him to understand me, to tell me it was okay, to tell me I wasn't wrong, to tell me he was there for me. I needed comfort and support. I needed him. My spiritual father.

I started to beat myself up. I should not have allowed myself to be so vulnerable, I should not have poured out my emotions and heart to him. Tears trickled down my face, and I felt lost. Who should I turn to now? What should I do? It was hard, horrid, and surreal. He explained that no marriage was perfect, which I knew, but it did not help how I felt. The marriage I was in was killing me. I'm sure not every marriage came with that feeling, and if it did – wow! If that was the case, then I didn't want to be married – what was the point? I know marriages have problems. I know there are often a lot of problems in the first year of marriage, but we didn't have first year marriage problems. We didn't have problems about making the bed, sleeping early/late, or taking shoes off at the door. The problems we had messed with my emotions, my head, my thinking. There is a big difference between abuse and disagreements. They are not the same. Abuse is not a disagreement.

One of the most difficult things during my healing process was knowing who would not only listen to me, but understand me. My emotions were everywhere. It was not just about the emotional abusive relationship now, it was becoming something much bigger.

It felt like a punishment from God. It felt like God had just turned his back on me. I was completely isolated and abandoned. What Pastor Daniel had said hurt so much. It was the sort of pain one would feel if a sword was going through a bone. All I could see was blackness. I wanted an escape. I needed an escape. I screamed and shouted. I shouted at my mum for allowing me to get into this, for seeing me through the suffering, for not saving me. I shouted and screamed to myself. I was angry. I needed to get out. I needed to run away.

My friend Tanisha had been at my house. She was there from early afternoon and had been there when I had the conversation with Pastor Daniel in the evening. She had watched me go from 0 to 100, physically and mentally. I couldn't contain myself, all I kept thinking was the conversation I had with Pastor Daniel. I kept hearing his words that he regretted joining Nick and I together.

I cried to her. She hugged me and told me it was okay. I did not want to hear that. It was not okay, nothing was okay. I screamed. My mum called my sister to come round to calm me down. She came but I didn't calm down, I couldn't; it was all so fresh. All I could think was: where is my escape?

I tried to run away. Physically. I stood up and ran to the door, it was 10 p.m. at night. It was pitch black outside. I didn't know where to go. I just needed to run away. Tanisha stopped me. My mum stopped me. I continued to try to get out. I held onto Tanisha getting her out of my way. She stood firm by the door. 'You are not going anywhere,' she said.

My mum was worried. She cried. She didn't know what to do. She called my aunty, who came round with my cousin. Later that evening, Pastor Kenny also came round. I don't know how I felt about her being there. It was now 11:30 p.m. and the situation was becoming worse as the whole year and a half played on my mind along with Pastor Daniel's words. I couldn't think clearly, and I continued to try to run away. My cousin and aunty stood by the door. Tanisha and Jacklyn tried to hold me down. All I wanted to do was run, run as fast as I could, in the dark, in the cold, as the wind blew and let fate take its course. I didn't want life anymore. I wanted to escape from the feelings of hurt, betrayal and sadness. There were a lot of feelings I felt. I don't know where they came from. It was as if they came one by one. Every time they came, I shouted it out loud, 'I feel dirty, ashamed, disgusted, sad, depressed...' The list went on. We were all sat in the living room. Everyone silent and listening to me. My aunty told me to let it all out. I did. I screamed so loud I'm sure the neighbours four houses down and across the road would have heard me.

2 a.m. in the morning, I found myself sitting in A&E.

The doctor asked me how I felt. All I said was that I was tired. Emotionally tired. Tired of crying, tired of the arguments, tired of being told I was the problem for everything. Tired of everything. I didn't know what else to say. The doctor explained that he saw many patients, and it was usually easy to decide what happened next, but with me, he was unsure. He said my responses had made him wary. He allowed me space to talk about how I felt, the marriage, the pregnancy, everything. He gave me time, and he gave me space. I was grateful.

He asked whether I wanted to stay in the hospital or go home, but I was unsure what to do. All I wanted to do was to sit on the chair and not go anywhere.

I explained to him that I would stay in the hospital. He explained that they could give me medication – anti-depressants – but what he thought I truly needed was counselling. I also agreed, but I agreed to take the medication for now.

He gave me a medicine that would help put me to sleep. I took it, and in a few moments, I was asleep. Jacklyn was also there with me in the room, and I was grateful she stayed. I appreciated her for being there with me that night.

Going home the next morning, I left with the anti-depressants and sleeping tablets, which I was encouraged to take every day. A member of the home treatment team visited me every morning to see if I was okay. I was happy that I could speak and share how I felt without being judged. It was the first time in a while that I could just share my thoughts, feelings, and experiences without having to hide. However, it was obvious they were also coming to check that I was still taking my medication.

The anti-depressants did not completely work. I needed to talk, and the more I talked, the more I healed. I would ask when I could stop taking the anti-depressants, and was told, 'Take them for another six months, and then we can see how to wean you off,' the lady from the home treatment team said. She continued, 'It's not good to stop taking them suddenly.'

I felt trapped. What was going on? What would happen to me if I didn't take them? I knew I didn't need them; I was happy now. Nick had gone, and I was free. I stopped taking the anti-depressants and replaced it with Holy Communion, the blood and body of Jesus. I covered myself with the blood of Jesus and prayed I would not stay depressed.

A few days later, I decided to tune into evening prayers on Zoom. I'm not really sure why. I guess I wanted to be in the presence of God and experience the peaceful feeling I always had before. I had joined when Pastor Daniel was praying: 'We need to pray for our marriages. The enemy is out to destroy marriages. The enemy is out to destroy homes. Everyone! Pray! Pray! Pray!!!' he exclaimed. I could see those with their cameras on praying: some were standing, some were sitting. They were shaking their heads. It looked like serious prayers were taking place.

I sat completely still, looking at the screen, camera off, of course. He then mentioned that the focus for the next three days will be on marriages due to 'the enemy breaking homes.' I sat and listened for 15 minutes then switched it off. I wondered if it had been because of the situation between Nick and I. Our broken marriage.

I understand the fact that the enemy is breaking homes, however, it didn't sit right with me. Not now anyway. The enemy breaking homes and me being emotionally abused was too separate things. Unless, in fact, the enemy caused Nick to behave like that? Gosh! It was too much. My mind was racing with thoughts. I put on some worship music and fell asleep.

Chapter 16

Taking Back Control

I started a six-month course called 'Taking Back Control', a course in which I would learn about triggers, early warning signs, and not falling into the traps. I was shocked at how life had completely turned around, but I was happy. I was pulling myself together. I started to really enjoy the course. There were five other women there, and the trainers were both men.

How did I get there? How did this happen to me? I stopped asking myself these questions. This could easily happen to someone who was so in love with a best friend from school, or a love at first sight. People change, and situations occur. Jas, just thank God you were strong enough to walk away, or rather, to kick him out. I was strong. I was brave, I told myself.

From the course, I learned about therapeutic activities that help to focus the mind; colouring was one. With the determination to move on with my life and recover as fast as I could, the first thing I did when I got home was to order an adult colouring book and pastel colouring pencils. They arrived the next day, and I got into it straight away. My son was on one side of the bed, and I lay there, colouring on the other. It was wonderful and perfect. My mind focused, trying to make sure I stayed between the lines. Colouring is a powerful tool for reducing stress and anxiety. It has the ability to calm the fear centre in the brain. It generates a sense of calm and reduces thoughts in a racing mind. It was great.

I was excited to go back to the course the following week to share what I had been doing with the others, and I started to really enjoy the course.

Topic five was on triggers; this was powerful.

'I will leave the door open. If it gets too much, please feel free to walk out for a break,' the trainer said in a soft, calm tone. *Wow!* I thought. I was excited and nervous at the same time as to what I might experience. Would I be the one to walk through the door with my head down? Would I be the one who was unable to handle the topic? The one to get caught in my own situation to the point where I would need to have to break from it all?

We had to write down what our triggers were. If there was anyone, any topics or conversations that would release an overload of negative neurons in the body. What caused a surge of anger, sadness, anxiety, a heavy heart, and tense shoulders?

I began to write. 'The church,' I wrote as trigger one. I couldn't believe I had written that, but I knew I cared so much about the church, and if I heard something about the situation or my getting back with Nick, I might be upset and unhappy.

Point two: I put his name. I couldn't avoid him; at that point, he was a trigger. I didn't want to write it on the page. I wanted to feel as though he didn't affect me, but Jas, let's be real: he is a trigger. I wrote down his name, scribbling it on the page. I could not believe that just writing his name down would be a challenge, as if me writing his name was me still connecting with him. I did not want to become bitter and cold, hateful and vengeful. I just wanted to heal.

The next section was how to deal with these triggers. I began writing 'colouring' for every point. Whenever a trigger came up, I would take out my colouring book, put on some worship music, and colour. It helped. It really did help. Of course, when a trigger popped up, I wasn't always calm enough to say, 'Oh, I will colour now,' but after the situation had settled, and I picked up the colouring book, I felt relaxed.

Had I sinned? Had I done wrong in God's eyes? I was sad. All I wanted to do was God's will. I just wanted to walk straight down the path God had for me, holding His hand during the journey. Was I wrong for not staying and enduring the emotions? Standing strong, always praying for peace of mind – had I given up too early? Should I have continued for years until I couldn't continue anymore? I had so many thoughts but the very thought that popped up in a silent still state was: 'Jasmine, you have done the right thing.'

Many women stay for years upon years. Sometimes it takes 20 years of marriage before they finally decide they can no longer be a victim. No. No. No. I did not want that.

He never hit me, he hadn't cheated, but we were not married long enough to know what could have happened; however, I did not want to wait for the emotional turmoil to lead me into the pit of enflamed fire. I had had enough.

I couldn't believe I was a single mum, but at the same time, it felt better than the constant tears of unhappiness, the belief that I was always wrong, the gaslighting, being told I had anger issues, and crying all night. It was better than all of that.

I still wonder though, had he married me for papers? It didn't make sense. Surely if he did, he would have waited until after he had received his papers to treat me how he treated me. Surely, he wouldn't have shown his true self at the very beginning? I cannot say for sure whether he did or did not, but speaking to a few people about the situation, they seem to believe that he had. He had just married me for papers. A part of me still thinks it was a little more than just papers. Nevertheless, it's a thought to ponder on.

Someone who saw my weakness but wanted to help me grow, someone who would help me, who would bring out the better side of me – that was who I wanted. I'd left the marriage, but I felt happy. The voices telling me that God was no longer with me came up several times, but I realised that so many women, so many of God's children, may have previously experienced a divorce, a broken marriage, children outside of marriage, and it made me know that God still had me in his hand. God still loved his daughter, his child, and he would still be close to me; oh, so close. He would still bless me. He wouldn't suddenly abandon me.

Nick was still a leader at the church, and I had been informed that he was leading the live Bible Study session one evening. Pastor Kenny called my mum to tell her that Nick would be leading Bible study on Tuesday and that my mum should pass the message on to me, and if I didn't want to tune in, I didn't have to. When my mum brought the message to me, I was shocked and devastated. I enjoyed all church services and loved attending Bible study. I had made a commitment that I would always tune in and be a part of the service, so I was heartbroken to hear they were still allowing him to teach, and now I couldn't be a part of it. So we left the church, my mum, Zian and I. The whole situation made me think about the system, not just church, but the wider community. Why is there no action taken or consequences for husbands who abuse their wives? There's no discipline or penalty for what they have done or the damage they have caused? Nick continued to teach in Sunday School, which I struggled to understand. How and why was this still happening? It made me wonder whether I was seen as the one who did the wrong. After all, I did call the police on him. Why is it so often that the woman and the children are the ones to leave the community, the area, the home or the church? Why could she not stay, and the abuser leave? I pondered on this for a few days trying to understand what is beyond my understanding.

Although we left, we were connected to another church through a counselling line. We attended that Sunday and although it was great, I cried. I didn't want to leave my previous church. Why could they not understand? Why couldn't Nick leave, and I continue attending? Why did it have to be so difficult? Leaving Nick was one thing and leaving the church was another. I'd wished it had been simpler.

I had to encourage and motivate myself as much as I could. *Surely God knows and understands exactly what happened? God knows the truth and sees my heart, all will be okay. You are not bad at all, Jas, and this is not your fault.* I told myself this often. I certainly needed to hear it. There were not many people reaching out to me from my previous church which was really sad, however, I hadn't reached out to anyone. I didn't really know who to talk to, who would understand? I wondered whether they would tell me to go back to Nick and that I was wrong or that I shouldn't let the enemy win, that I should pray and fight for my marriage. With everything going on, I appreciated God for keeping me strong.

I also thank those who did encourage me, who told me I had done the right thing and who explained their stories to me.

'It's good it happened now, sweetie,' an aunty said. 'I was married for 18 years and accepted the physical, emotional, and financial abuse. It's now ten years later, and I wish I had been brave like you, not to suffer in silence, not to fear people, family, and the unknown. Well done! I am proud of you.'

It was so encouraging to hear those very words: 'well done', 'you are brave', and 'I am proud of you'. It made me know that although some people looked at me side-eyed, others were, in fact, inspired by me. It was reassuring to know that what I had done was perfectly fine and accepted by others. Even if it was not accepted by others, I did not care but it was very encouraging to know it was. I knew I wanted happiness, and I was willing to look like the horrible person to be able to have it. Life is way too often fake. We post on social media, we say, 'Yes, we are doing well,' but we don't speak out and tell people how we are suffering. We don't tell the truth, and we are not honest with ourselves. I was far from that feeling now – I was being honest and transparent. I needed to speak up.

I had not lost my sense of self entirely, but I knew that if the marriage had continued without a change, it would have gone down a road I could never have dreamed of. Imagine losing your sense of self without a single mark or bruise – no one would ever know. Those wounds are invisible to others, hidden in self-doubt, worthlessness, and self-loathing. Research indicates that the dramatic effect emotional abuse has on its victims and its consequences are just as severe as those from physical abuse. I was created to have emotional freedom, divine peace within, and strong self-esteem. Emotional abuse, unfortunately, undermines God's purpose for an individual's life, but what encouraged me was that what others have sabotaged and abandoned, God can strengthen and rebuild.

I was encouraged, I was happy, and I was filled with a feeling of relief. It was the feeling of finally having my life back – not a sane life or a new life with my son, but a good life in which I was at peace. Nick and I were not legally married, due to his papers, we had only done the church vows and received the blessing from Pastor Daniel, so there was no paperwork for the divorce. It took me some time to get my head around this – Nick and I were not legally married. It was not real. He was not really my husband. I believe not having to go through a divorce helped me heal a lot quicker. I can't imagine what it would have been like going through the documents and paperwork, filing for the divorce, whilst being a new mum and juggling motherhood. Although it wasn't easy, I am grateful, it wasn't as hard as it could have been. Looking at the darkest tunnel, there is always a reason to give thanks because a few roads down, there is an even darker tunnel that you are not going through.

As time went on, I felt as if I needed to share my story. I had an app on my phone called Peanut – an app for women to come together. On the app, there was a podcast section where anyone could start a podcast about anything. I noticed that some women started Christian podcasts, and I was encouraged to take steps to start one myself. That was the beginning of my speaking up to share my story. Many women messaged me after I'd shared my testimony. Some said they were going through the same thing and needed help. Some said they had gone through it and had also left. Others were encouraged and felt lifted. I was amazed at the responses of women all around the world who had been encouraged by my story. Survivors and victims from all different backgrounds were reaching out to me, sharing their stories. It was powerful. I was happy that I could give back. I didn't go through all of that for nothing, I told myself. Sometimes, we go through situations, not for ourselves but for someone else to encourage and help someone else through her situation. I was encouraged. Really encouraged, but I was also sad to see so many women afraid to speak out and seek help. I wanted a microphone. I wanted to go louder. I wanted to empower and encourage as many women as I could. I thought about all the different channels I could go down, from TED talks to the Oprah Winfrey Show. I wanted to be a voice, a voice for women. *If I could get into that marriage and go through that, there was nothing I could not do*, I thought. I had gained a power and strength I never knew I had. I could do anything I wanted with God on my side. I was going further than I could imagine. I was still nervous and would sometimes cry, but I continued to encourage myself and share my story. I continued to share my journey, and I was happy I had been set free. I could see how the experience I went through was more a gift than a curse because not only do I have my son, but I learned how to channel it into some of the greatest victories of my life.

Chapter 17

New Era

As the weeks went by, I got more strength. I was starting a new job in September. A teacher training position. I had always wanted to become a teacher from when I was a child. The idea of teaching gives me great joy. It's my passion. This was now my opportunity, and I was extremely excited to embark on not only what was a start of a new me but also me finally fulfilling my purpose. As I was waiting on September, I enjoyed the new life I had. Day by day, I went to Mummy and Baby groups and made new friends with other mums. I was always open about my trauma and what I had been through. Telling my story was a way for me to heal. Leaving the house in the morning to make it to the 11 a.m Mummy and Baby group, I was finding stability in everyday life. I planned my days and prepared myself for the start of a new beginning. I made plans to go out with Zian; sometimes just the two of us, sometimes with another mum and child. On some days, I would take him to another town. Being a baby of three or four months meant that he was usually always fast asleep. I didn't mind. I enjoyed pushing the pushchair and seeing him sleep peacefully.

It was not easy at times. I would often reflect and work on coming to terms with what had happened. I still tried my best to look forward, ready to start on something new.

Parenting as a single mum wasn't easy. Zian would wake up two to three times in the night. I was often extremely exhausted due to lack of sleep. But I didn't mind. In a sense I, rather liked it. He needed me. I needed him.

I knew I wanted to do more. I knew I was not just a mum. I was more. I just wanted to become the best version of me that I could be.

One sunny afternoon, sitting thinking about what I could do, I decided to search for a women business networking event. I was thinking about business ideas, and although I had nothing really set in action yet, I decided to explore.

I found a woman in business event online. It looked good and before I knew it, I had ordered my ticket and was getting ready to go the following week.

I was slightly nervous about going as I hadn't been to an event like that before. However, I was excited to do something new. The new perception I had about life was something I had never experienced. Life is full of opportunities to take advantage of and there had been so many times I had let them pass me by.

The morning of the event, I woke up early to prepare my son to stay with my mum before preparing myself for the networking event. The venue was a distance away and driving in London can be a little crazy, so I got public transport. It was the first time that I had taken public transport since I was married! In all honesty, I felt free again!

As I got dressed in the morning, I put make up on and found a cute but formal outfit to wear. *I deserved to feel great* I thought. What I went through was not who I am. I was happy with myself. *Well done you Jas,* I said to myself as I put on my shoes.

Taking public transport was a pleasant experience which I actually really enjoyed. Although everyone was wearing masks, I really felt a sense of community. As I looked at the different passengers getting on and off the bus, I thought about where they were going or where they were coming from. I thought about what story they may have, what life was offering them. I knew what I was going through. What was going on for them? Everyone has a story. Everyone has something going on whether positive or negative. There was a family that walked onto the bus, a man, a woman and two children. I reckon they were husband and wife. I looked to see if they were wearing rings. I couldn't help but think and wonder whether the lady was happy. It sounds bizarre, but I knew exactly how it could be – you look happy, all looks okay, but really it's an entirely different situation behind closed doors. I watched and pondered. I couldn't help but hope that she was okay, praying she was happy and enjoying her relationship. I sent her all good wishes and her children too.

The bus journey was busy, but I enjoyed it. I couldn't help but smile underneath my face mask. I had reconnected with ordinary life. Finally. I got to the event and met with the other women; I must have been the youngest I reckoned. Nevertheless, we all got talking. Honestly, you know the feeling you have when you are just proud of yourself? I had that feeling.

Within a few minutes, we were sat around the table, ready for the lunch networking event to begin. The host, bless her, Sally, started by welcoming us all. She gave a warm welcome to me and another lady. We were new. It was then I realised all the other women knew each other and the event takes place every month.

'I am so grateful we are here again in person. Although we were getting used to the virtual sessions, it feels good to be back,' she said with a smile on her face.

Everyone else nodded and smiled. There was a real sense of community amongst the women. I could feel the love circulating in the room.

'I think we should go round and say one thing we are grateful for,' Sally continued.

She went first and we went around the table. It was a phenomenal moment. The atmosphere was filled with gratitude and thanksgiving. It nearly brought tears to my eyes.

As I sat there, I wondered what I would say. Should I tell them that I was in an emotional abusive marriage and I left? No, I can't. But that is what I'm truly grateful for and my son of course. *If I do say it, I'm going to cry*

I thought to myself. I even started crying at the thoughts in my head. How could I hold it together saying it out loud to strangers?

Jasmine, think fast, think real fast! It was now time; I was speaking next and as I started, I knew no one would expect what was to come.

'Firstly, thank you for having me here today. I am extremely grateful for this moment. I am also grateful because…' as I was speaking the room went silent. All eyes were on me. I could see the women smiling at me. I knew they would not expect this.

'I'm grateful because last year, March 2020, the beginning of the lockdown, I got married and..' they had already started clapping.

'Oohh congratulations!' a few said.

'Unfortunately not. It was an emotionally abusive relationship, and I guess what I want to say is, I am so grateful because just a few months ago, I said *no*, I said *no* to the abuse, and I left the situation. I now have a baby. My son and I couldn't be more grateful that I had the strength to leave.' Tears started to pour down my face. 'I'm sorry, I know I'm crying, but truly I am grateful. I am truly thankful. Thank you so much.' A lady passed me a tissue whilst they all clapped again.

'Jasmine, I know we are just meeting for the first time, but wow, I am so proud of you!' a lady said. 'Many women don't have the strength to do what you did.' 'Please know that we are not just a community of women in business, but we are also a support group, and we are here to support you,' another said.

It was lovely and although I had cried, I knew…I knew that I had overcome.

I did it, I thought inside. I spoke publicly about what I had been through, not on a podcast, not on the phone, but in person. This was now becoming more real.

This was the beginning of something new. It was now time for me to channel all my courage into healing and getting back to being a happy, healthy, and whole me.

There were a few days where I felt sad and down, but I recognised it and knew it was important to allow myself to experience the feelings and to let them out, rather than bottling them up, which I had tried to do on some occasions. I mean even mentioning or hearing his name would make me uneasy.

To better regulate my emotions and my understanding of everything I had been through, I started journaling. Writing allowed me to restore a sense of power over my life. Whilst writing on several occasions, it reminded me of my strengths and that indeed I am capable of creating. Whenever any thoughts came to my mind, I picked up my journal and wrote it all down. *Write it down girl. Write it all*, I would say to myself. Through my words, I was breaking the cycle my mind would take me on when I remembered the past and rewrote the script of my life. I kept writing and reassessing my way into restoring a better life, whilst sharing my story to help others know they are not alone, can speak up, and have peace after abuse and trauma.

Being able to sit with, process, and understand my thoughts, feelings, and behaviours was part of my healing experience.

I'd spent countless hours in prayer in my personal study, learning everything I could about abuse and – even more importantly – how to heal.

As September due nearer, I was drawing closer to the start of the academic year and I had to get things sorted and make sure things were in place. Ultimately, my mind and my peace.

I had to set my boundaries and the no contact continued. Nick and I managed to set up a plan not directly talking, but through mediation, so he could still arrange visits with Zian. The mediation was on Zoom and I requested for a type of mediation called 'shuttle.' This was for those who wanted protection having been in an abusive relationship. Therefore, Nick and I never saw each other. Whilst he was speaking with the mediator, I was in the waiting room and then we would switch. It was now five months since I had seen him or spoken to him. I think the no contact is an amazing boundary where I could take back some control. It was my decision, and no one could force me to speak to him. It really wasn't necessary. Even with a child, there was a way. It reminded me of an old Christian song; *He Made a Way*. God will always make a way. Scripture says He makes a way in the wilderness and in the desert. Surely God made a way for me.

As the days went on, I worked on retraining my brain and mind. Instead of seeing him as the man he was to me, I rather viewed him as Zian's father. Someone who shared Zian's life with me, but he was no longer invited to peer into the rest of my life. To also retrain my brain and my mind, I declared healing affirmations in the morning and evening. Daily, I told myself:

I am free.

He no longer has control over me.

I am beautiful and I am whole.

Unfortunately, it wasn't just the marriage that made me sad, it was everything that happened with the church. Honestly, it was as if that church and I had the breakup. Sometimes it was hard to process as I thought about the lack of support and help from the church. That took more time to get over, seriously. I found myself thinking about it for hours. I, however, had to get on and practise all the techniques I had been learning. I had to fight hard to move past this.

I had support; I found my tribe. I surrounded myself with a close-knit community of people in my life that validated, supported, and protected me. I am extremely grateful. Owning my wounds and recognising the part of myself that needed attention and healing, I was standing tall. I wasn't all the way healed, but I was a lot closer to it than I could have imagined half a year ago. Eventually, I started to see a therapist so that I could gain the strength and courage to move on.

I had gone to a church conference with mum and Zian. A graduation was taking place. The church had a bible college, and many students were graduating. They walked onto the stage whilst everyone clapped for them. Just like teaching, I had always wanted to do bible college. It was something I had had on my mind since I was 18 years old, and I couldn't help but think I really want to be next to graduate. Once the graduation had finished, the minister mentioned the steps to sign up for the next bible college. It was starting very soon. My mind raced as I thought about how I could do both teacher training and bible college whilst also looking after my son. The minister then mentioned that the bible college sessions are in the evening, and online. *Well that makes it possible*, I thought. I will register, God will make a way and I will be able to do both.

As soon as I got home, I registered and, within two weeks, I had enrolled onto the bible college course. I was more than grateful. The teaching was going great and although I sometimes was very tired during the evening lectures, I loved it. I loved every moment.

As the weeks went on, I realised the moments of genuine happiness had changed to hours, followed by days, then followed by periods where I didn't even think about Nick or the situation at all.

I still don't know what love is – love between husband and wife or a couple for that matter, but I know it's not warm and fuzzy feelings. It's actions. It's what you do rather than what you say. Relationships are not supposed to be like a cat and mouse chase. One of the subtleties of an abusive relationship is the dynamic of 'Come here. Go away,' or 'I love you so much. I don't love you at all.'

I still want to love and be loved, but in all honesty, men scare me a little. It's going to be a special guy who takes my guard down – who will be patient with me, genuinely patient with me. I know one day I will meet him but there is no rush at all.

The teacher training programme required me to also enrol in university to complete my teacher qualification. I would teach in a school Monday to Friday with a training session on Thursday at the university. Honestly, it was extremely busy at times, but I knew I could do it. Deep within me, I knew I was on the right path. For the first time in a long time, things were shifting into the right place.

It also kept me busy with little to no time thinking about the past. I loved teaching – the profession where you are mindful and present in the moment. I love the fact that whilst teaching you can't plan and whilst planning you can't teach. You have to be present either planning, teaching or marking. My favourite moment will always be the 50 minutes where I would teach the class. That was my joy. Whilst I was at work, my mum helped look after Zian. It gave me peace. I knew he was okay. My weekends were my time to connect with Zian. I enjoyed it. It was my absolute pleasure. I looked forward to the weekends.

I will complete my teacher training and graduate from bible college in a few months. I cannot wait.

As the days and weeks continued, I continued to write and after some months, my writing transformed into this book you hold in your hands right now.

Chapter 18

The Signs

People often ask me: couldn't you see the signs before? Yes, I did, but I was so focused on the fact that it had been God's will for my life. I had cried so many times at work because we had argued via text message because our plans for the wedding weren't the same. I was told that I couldn't speak to my mum, that I couldn't express my feelings to her. This was a big warning sign because any daughter, any child, should be able to speak with his or her parents before they go into a marriage. I was suddenly walking on eggshells around my mum: 'Mum, I'm telling you this, but please, don't tell Nick that I told you. He wouldn't be happy I did it.' I never stopped talking to my mum. In fact, I told her everything. It continued into the marriage, especially given the way Nick had treated me. I had to speak to her. I had to speak to someone. She was my encourager, a listening ear. Looking back now, any man who tells a woman she should not talk to her mum before they are married is a bad sign, a red flag.

As I started to heal, I researched as much as I could on narcissism and emotional abuse. Everything I read rang true. It was exactly what I had felt and had gone through. It all made sense. I was coming to terms with everything I had been through. Although I had received a few comments about going back to the marriage, I thought that there was no way I could go back. Would someone who had just healed from being burned in a fire walk back into the fire? Would someone who had just got onto the right path decide to turn around and go down the wrong path again? I knew I couldn't go back.

In my heart, I had forgiven Nick. I forgave him for how he had made me feel, for the upset and the trauma, but I was not able to see him yet to confront him. I had to be wise. God had healed me. I had become whole again. Not perfect, but whole. Trauma is personal.

I started counselling with my pastor, Pastor Philip. He helped me through the healing process. He recognised that I needed to heal from the trauma of the past, and he gave me scriptures on which to meditate and focus. He prayed with me and stood by me with encouragement and support, and I was very grateful. It was encouraging to have a Pastor behind me, supporting and praying with me as I unfortunately did not have that from the previous church. I knew God had not left me. There is a popular saying I would hear in church since I was a young child, 'Men may fail, but God would never.' It was only now I really understood the saying and meaning.

The next course I did was on Mindfulness. It was all about the mind, the thought process, and our thinking. It was about how we can control our thoughts, which was something I had never thought one was able to do. I was excited about the course. It was something I had never experienced, a study into the brain, a magnificent, beautiful creation. I started to research the brain and the thought process.

Eighty per cent of what we thought about yesterday is the same today. There are hardly any changes unless you make them. In the brain, there are pathways, and these pathways are being created every day. The more you think about something, the more you create the pathway. Learning all about the brain and the mind, I was able to help myself. Faith without work is dead, right? I had to do my part. I had to do something to help myself. When I would get angry at how this had all happened, I had to stop, pause, and reflect on something else instead. Energy follows thought, and I didn't want to give energy to negative thoughts. Not anymore. The course was powerful, and I could see the changes in me.

I was really enjoying the mindfulness course and the different practices we did together. There was a sense of openness and honesty in the group which was uplifting. On this occasion, the trainer spoke about the body scan practice, something I had never heard of before; it was all new to me.

During the body scan you bring attention to your body, noticing the different sensations as you mentally scan down, from head to toe. I thought of it as a laser copier scanning the length of my body. The body scan is a meditation practice to reduce the stress related ailments that one may experience. I was having back pain and headaches, although I think the backpain was a postpartum symptom and probably from the breastfeeding.

The trainer explained how the physical discomfort we experience is often due to our emotional state and the body scan is useful and effective at allowing us to check in with our bodies.

The idea of the practice is to stay present while breathing into the different sensations in the body. It brings relief to the mind by evolving our relationship to pain, aches, and discomfort. The purpose is to tune in to your body – to reconnect to your physical self – and notice any sensations you're feeling without judgement.

While many people find the body scan relaxing, the trainer explained that relaxation was not the primary goal. All in all, I was looking forward to it. I didn't know what to expect.

The goal of the scan is to train the mind to be more open and aware of sensory experiences – and ultimately, more accepting. She spoke about the added benefits of the practice which included improved sleep, increased self-compassion, greater self-awareness and stress relief. I needed this!

She started by saying, 'You can close your eyes if that's comfortable for you.'

I closed my eyes in a seated position with my feet firmly on the floor.

She continued, 'Notice your body seated wherever you're seated, feeling the weight of your body on the chair, on the floor.'

Her voice was soothing and calming. We all took a few deep breaths in and out.

'Notice your left foot on the floor, notice the sensations of your left foot touching the floor. The weight and pressure, vibration, heat.'

'Notice your right foot against the floor, pressure, pulsing, heaviness, lightness.'

She continued with the left leg and right leg; we were checking into every body part. My mind started to wander, and it wasn't long before I started to feel extremely emotional. It was as if all the pain I had experienced came back. As she continued, I knew I needed to stop the practice. I knew I couldn't do any more, although I did try. My mind was pulling me so strongly that it was extremely hard to concentrate. Eventually I had to stop. I opened my eyes. She recognised, nodded and smiled at me, whilst continuing for the others. I looked around and wondered why no one else had experienced the same emotions. The others were still deeply in the practice. I sat and waited.

'Be aware of your whole body as best you can. Take a breath. And then when you're ready, you can open your eyes,' she said in a soft voice to the rest of the group. *Finally*! I thought.

We always gave feedback after our practices and this time I was eager and intrigued to see how the others found it. Had I been the only one that couldn't handle the practice?

The others had found it relaxing and beneficial. I was surprised. When it was my turn, I expressed how it made me feel. 'I will never do this practice again,' I said, whilst laughing. She explained that this practice may not be good for anyone who is dealing with emotional trauma as emotions that have been suppressed can become released during the body scan meditation. I was relieved. She had made sense of what I was experiencing. She explained that often people with pain from emotional trauma may take a step back from this practice and revisit another time.

'It gets easier with time,' she said. Whether or not I would do the scan again, I wasn't sure. I just knew, at that moment, it was not for me. The rest of the session was good. We did a different practice. A much shorter one. It was better. I enjoyed it.

I bought a dozen books on mindfulness. I read day and night. Any time I had a second from mummy duties, I picked up a book and read. I wanted to know all I could know about the brain and the mind so I could heal and I could heal quicker. I didn't want years to pass, and I was still making terms with the trauma, the upset, the sadness. I refused. I needed to heal, and now. I needed to move forward, and now. I read many books, and what stood out was a book I read called *Dear Life* by Rachel Clarke, a book about a doctor who works with the terminally ill. It made me appreciate the beauty around me, and it made me value life. It helped me to change my thought process and to heal.

Six weeks later, and I had completed the course on mindfulness. I could see the impact, the recovery, the strength, the power being ignited, being lifted, and I knew my life was changing. I was becoming.

I had finally become empowered in my thoughts, my actions, my mind, and my life. The subconscious mind is extremely powerful, and whilst it would remind me of the hurt and trauma I had experienced, I was able to free myself from that bondage. Finally, I was stronger, my head was held high, and I no longer felt weak and incapable of doing anything. God had strengthened me. God had helped. Thank you, Jesus.

I had that powerful, can-do anything spirit. I found reservoirs of strength I never knew I had. I thought to myself that if I could go into a marriage with a man I didn't love, but I was willing to make it work, if I could go through the emotional turmoil and still come out the other end, then I could do anything. Often, we shy away from opportunities, from change, from something new due to fear, due to the strange fear of accepting the unknown but going into opportunities builds you as a person. It gives you strength. You will begin to go through life with new experiences, with added qualities.

For my son, the joy that had come from the relationship, I am grateful. Seeing my son, a very happy little boy, I am at peace, and I am happy. I have a beautiful, handsome gift from above. A treasure. A love. Looking at him, every time I have peace. Happy mum, happy baby – it's truly precious. I am grateful for the refined woman I am, for the wings God has given me, not only to fly but to fly high. I am a new person, saying yes to new opportunities and saying yes to life. I thank God for all the new opportunities that have come from this and urge you, dear reader, if you are in a time of new beginnings or a time of waiting, in a period in which you feel lost, worried, or anxious, say yes to something new. No, that does not mean entering a marriage with someone you don't know, but it does mean being ready to push yourself more than you are capable.

One of the most remarkable elements of my healing journey was the powerful knowledge I gained along the way. I could see how overcoming the marriage changed me, giving me a completely new perspective on life. Sitting in the sauna, I spoke with a woman. 'Why don't you go under the ice-cold bucket after the sauna?' she asked.

'Oh, no, not me,' I replied.

'It's great for your body. Athletes do it when they train.' She went on about how great it was and how she did it every day.

It's too cold for me, I thought, I will stick to what I know, nice and hot. As I came out of the sauna and was walking towards the shower, I saw the ice bucket hanging, waiting to be pulled. Instantly, it came to me: *Jas, if you can marry Nick and come out of the emotional turmoil, honey, you can do anything.* I went straight underneath the bucket and pulled the rope.

Cold. Shivers. Relief.

The ice-cold water touched my face, my arms, my back. I stood in the moment, not thinking about anything. I was just in absolute awe. *This is awesome!* I thought. I had never thought I would have done anything like that before. That was the moment I knew I could do anything. Ever since, I have continued to use the ice bucket whenever I go to the gym. There is something so powerful when you believe in yourself, and you do not let a situation or circumstance define you. Although you cannot change the past, you can shape the future.

Chapter 19

Freedom

I joined private support groups on emotional and narcissistic abuse and realised that thousands of women and even men were suffering. People would ask questions and leave posts about the relationships they were trying to leave or the relationships they had left. Some had been with their partners for five years, some 15, some 20, some longer. I couldn't believe my ears. Some had left and kept going back. That was when I came across what is known as trauma bond, when the victim continues to go back to his/her abuser only to leave again and again. It typically continues over years until the victim decides s/he is finally done.

I didn't have that. I couldn't understand the meaning – why would anyone go back to feeling low and depressed? Had I been lucky? Was it because I didn't actually love him? Had I had an easy escape, or was it my determination and strong zeal not to live a fake life and be unhappy? I don't know; I do know that I was not ever going to go back into that situation. I was ready for whatever life wanted me to face, and I wrote this book to encourage all women – or really, anyone – going through what I did to tell them that life does get better.

I met a lady through the support group named Dianna. She was married for 34 years and had been separated for seven. She expressed how she hadn't realised what was wrong with her for 34 years, all of which she believed she had low self-esteem, anxiety, and depression. She explained, 'I knew I was tired, confused, and I'd had enough.' She went to a therapist and explained what she had been feeling and that she now felt flat emotionally, just like I had been. Dianna was almost 60, and she spoke about the feeling of being free; I now understood that feeling, one of freedom and peace.

I read about her story and was happy for her, happy for the thousands of women who say no, and in all, I was happy for myself.

God bless Louise, who allowed me to share her story. Louise had been married to Harry for 23 years. He had been her best friend since university, where they met. She explained that the man she had married – or the man she had thought she'd married – never truly existed. She expected to have a loving home and family and be married to him until death do them part, but she realised he was covertly abusing her, and her life shattered. Unfortunately, she was twice forcibly hospitalised for suicidal threats. He was a covert psychopath, and although they'd had years of counselling, he never changed. She explained how the church and community had failed her. She'd been betrayed by close Christian friends and family who, unfortunately, sided with him. The Bible also became a weapon used against her, with scriptures explaining how she had done everything wrong. She had one friend, however, who was able to sit with her and pour light and truth on her situation.

She saw a therapist for a year and recovered and healed from the effects the abuse had caused, and she had to rebuild herself and the way she saw herself, so she was not the paranoid, depressed, overreacting woman she once believed she was.

She explained that through her journey, she was free from the bondage of legalistic conservative Evangelicalism and found Jesus, the Almighty loving God. He held her close and taught her about what true love and acceptance really was. She started a support group and encouraged women from all around the world, including me. Thank you, Louise.

I am grateful for those I met on my journey. It was not easy, reaching out to people, only to feel abandoned and discounted, but those who understood – although not many at first – was comforting.

I am praying for you, the reader, that if you are or you know someone who is experiencing emotional abuse, may peace – divine peace, peace from above – fill you and them. You do not need to stay because of fear – people will talk about you whether you do good or bad, and that is the simple truth about life. Pleasing one person might upset another, but there is nothing we can do about it. We cannot please everyone. You must do what is right for you. Sometimes, this is how we shine in the darkness. Other people's miseries won't be remembered more than anything you could have suffered. The damage and invisible scars of emotional abuse are very difficult to heal. Memories are imprinted on our minds and hearts, and it takes time to be restored, but God, our comfort and healer, will restore you back to your sound mind and divine peace.

I thank God for making a way, for opening a door, for setting me free.

I'm not sad that I married him; I have no regrets. I believe that God is with me. I believe he will never leave nor forsake me. All in all, God sees me through. I thank God for my strength. I thank God for my healing. I thank God for seeing me through. Thank you, Lord. I am a survivor and a warrior. I am healing and thriving and transcending more and more every single day. I will get through whatever battle may come my way. I will push through. I now embrace myself as a whole, healthy, divine human being, worthy of love, compassion, and respect and I pray that you do, too.

Epilogue

This is my story, a chapter in my life, a time when I was living in what could be described as a twilight zone. It was a walk into the world of mental health, into a new life, of recovering from an emotionally abusive relationship, a marriage full of narcissistic behaviour and actions. I hope this has encouraged you as the reader, whether you are going through something similar to me, whether it is completely different, or whether you don't have a story at all. I pray this blesses you and touches your heart. This is life. There is a path to healing. I have chosen peace. I have chosen happiness. I have chosen joy. For myself and my son, I have survived things that have killed many others. My time of turmoil has come to an end. Having been dismissed, condemned, criticised, and shamed, my voice will not be silenced. My life is a message of hope.

About the Author

Mother of one, Jasmine Beverley is based in South London. She is passionate about empowering and encouraging women all around the world through the word of God. Her passion led her to launching a women's ministry, Daughters of Adonai, of which she is the founder and CEO.

She is a woman of strength, integrity, wisdom and a teacher of Mathematics. Jasmine Beverley has a tutoring company as she seeks for all children to excel in their studies no matter their upbringing and background. Her writing career started at the age of 26 when she felt she had a powerful message to share with the world.

To get in contact with Jasmine Beverley, you can contact her via:

Email: *jasminebeverleybooks@gmail.com*
Instagram: *@jasbeverley* or *@daughters_of_adonai*

Acknowledgements

I would like to express my appreciation and gratitude to my mum and stepdad for all the encouragement and support. Thank you for encouraging me not only to heal but to be greater than I was before. Thank you for believing in every dream I spoke out loud and for helping me to look after my son in the early stages of my healing.

In addition, I would like to thank both my sister and my brother for being supportive and listening ears whilst I shared my emotions and feelings.

To my son, you are my gift from God, and I love you always. Thank you

I am also thankful to family and friends for their support and comfort. I am eternally grateful to my pastor and therapist for the ongoing counselling they provided to help me get back to my normal self.

I am grateful to Daniella and every member of the team at Conscious Dreams Publishing for their ongoing support and hard work in bringing my story to life.

Furthermore, I am grateful to those, too many to name, who encouraged me to write this book to share my story.

My heartfelt appreciation goes to those who allowed me to share their stories. Your willingness to share your traumas will encourage and empower your fellow women. Thank you.

Above all, my deepest, heartfelt gratitude goes to God, who has given me the strength, comfort, and wisdom to write this book. It's a privilege I will never take for granted.

Thank you.

Lightning Source UK Ltd.
Milton Keynes UK
UKHW020946130422
401497UK00009B/175

9 781913 674908